An Insider's Guide to Currency Hedging and Conversions

You deserve to have insider information on how to develop the best hedging strategies and how to negotiate the best pricing for hedging and currency conversions

Ric Chappetto

An Insider's Guide to Currency Hedging and Conversions

An Insider's Guide to Currency Hedging and Conversions

Disclaimer

Copyright © 2020 Ric Chappetto

All Rights Reserved

No part of this Book may be reproduced, stored, or transmitted in any form or by any means, including mechanical or electronic, without prior written permission from the author.

While the author has made every effort to ensure that the ideas, statistics, and the information presented in this Book are accurate to the best of his abilities, any implications direct, derived, or perceived, should only be used at the reader's discretion. The author cannot be held responsible for any personal or commercial damage arising from communication, application, or misinterpretation of the information presented herein.

ISBN: 9798583546091

An Insider's Guide to Currency Hedging and Conversions

Foreword

Ric Chappetto is like Yoda to market participants. Not Baby Yoda, but not old Yoda, either. Let's call him "*Yoda in his prime*". With over 40 years in multiple markets, he has a unique understanding of not just the Foreign Exchange Market, but the intertwined nature of markets in general, as evidenced in the book. ***An Insider's Guide to Currency Hedging and Conversions*** reads like hedging for dummies, but minus the dummies part. The book is written for successful, intelligent business people who know they have been missing out on a key part of their growing international client base. Building a business is hard enough but being self-aware and humble enough to understand that you don't know what you don't know takes an extraordinary person. That's who reads this book. That's who **needs** this book.

The book is worth reading just for the comprehensive history of the United States currency, as it gives you insights into where we are now and how we got here. Then you start getting into foreign exchange terms, how the market trades, and why rates change, and you realize more than you did before, why you need this book. Ric details the 9 common types of risk in foreign exchange and breaks down each one of these in plain English. If you put this book down after reading that chapter, then you should probably pull back from your global dealings. I urge instead to push on as Ric describes exact strategies for managing these risks and others that may be unseen and are yet to come. He includes ideas to build your own program and develop strategies specific to your business.

You can't grow a business long-term without being global and until the world has one common currency (our great-great grandchildren have a shot at seeing this, but we don't), you will have currency risk. This book will introduce you to it, explain it in detail, and give you the framework for dealing with it. Ric's knowledge from his years of experience will make this comprehensive book the standard guide to hedging and conversions in the foreign exchange market. Read it twice.

Bob Iaccino

Bob Iaccino *spent the last 26 years in the stock, commodities, futures, and Foreign Exchange markets. He is a frequent guest analyst for Yahoo Finance, Bloomberg Television, CNBC, Fox News, Fox Business, CNN International, Cheddar TV, and AUSBIZ Daily, as well as providing analysis for the in-house networks of Charles Schwab and TD Ameritrade.*

Bob currently serves as the Co-Portfolio Manager of The Stock Think Tank, as well as the Co-Founder and Host of the PureXposure Growth Series, a live online investment show. Bob is also a founding principal and Chief Market Strategist of Path Trading Partners.

Table of Contents

Foreword	v
Introduction	1
Welcome to the World of Foreign Exchange	9
Introduction to the InterBank Market	13
Foreign Exchange Market Today	15
The History of the U.S. Currency	19
Foreign Exchange Terminology	31
How the Currency Market Trades	39
These 6 Factors Move the Market	51
Why Exchange Rates Change?	55
Key Indicators that Affect Currencies	59
Interest Rates and the Effect on Their Currencies	63
The Role of the US Dollar	67
Risk or Exposure	69
The 9 Common Foreign Exchange Risks	71
Strategies for Managing Currency Risk	79
Developing a Risk Management Program	81
Evaluating Risk before Entering a New Market	85
Understanding Hedging?	87
Developing Your Hedging Strategy	93

5 Hedging Instruments	99
Spot Market	101
Forward Contracts	109
Foreign Exchange Futures	117
Foreign Exchange Swaps	125
Foreign Exchange Options	129
Currency Correlations	141
Foreign Exchange Conversion – Delivery	145
Conclusion	157
Thank You	163
ABOUT THE AUTHOR	165

An Insider's Guide to Currency Hedging and Conversions

Introduction

Welcome to the very private world of Foreign Exchange

You made it past Bob's foreword, so you at least know that you do not know everything about the Foreign Currency Market and the best ways to use it to protect your profits. I wrote this book for you with the goal of providing the education needed to be a knowledgeable participant in the Foreign Exchange Market, not just a customer to a financial institution. Knowing how this market works will not only give you the confidence to challenge your banker or broker, but it will also give you the ability to question them in their terms, question their logic, and question the pricing behind their offer.

You will discover how different this market is compared to any other financial market you have used - from the size of the market ($5.4 trillion a day) to the trading environment, to the terminology used, to the way trades settle. Only then will you understand the complexities of this global market. With this knowledge, you will have the ability not only to better judge the proposals presented to you but also be able to offer your own strategy based on the multiple instruments you have to choose from, not just what your current institution has to sell.

By the end of this book, you might just feel a little naive about your past business transactions regarding currency hedging and currency conversions. That's fine, and in fact, a good sign because it means you're in a much better place now to deal with your future currency decisions.

The one thing that is important for you to remember as you read these **Case Studies** is that the people involved are successful businesspeople with years of experience. You will see that they never did anything wrong. They just did not have the knowledge to challenge what their institutional professionals told them to do. The companies they work for were all profitable and well respected in their industries. After we worked together, these people are now better prepared to execute these types of transactions. Their companies are more profitable, and that makes them respected even more.

Does the financial institution that performs your hedge or currency conversions say they do it at **"MARKET RATES"** and that they do not charge you anything? If they have said that they probably also told you that it is because you are such a great client, and it's a

"FREE SERVICE." However, the institution could have made $20,000 or more on that one transaction. Did they take the $20,000 or more ***"OUT-OF-THE-MARKET,"*** or did they take it ***"OUT-OF-YOUR-POCKET"***?

If you haven't hedged, or even if you have, did you ever wonder why when you looked into hedging your company's currency risk, it looks impossible to understand? Still, when you talk to your financial institution, they make it seem easy, as easy as signing a form, and you're done.

The reason they make it seem so easy is that they only present to you the product or products they sell. If you are lucky, their solution will be the one you need. If not, it will be the product you get.

I will show you how the two phrases ***"FREE SERVICE"*** and ***"MARKET RATE"*** can cost your firm anywhere from thousands of dollars to millions of dollars per year.

Using **Case Studies**, you will also learn from real-life events that I have been involved in. I will show you how I worked with a large, successful, fourth-generation, family-owned business doing millions of dollars a year with major US and Canadian companies. And I will explain how they could have their best sales year ever, yet something went wrong. Over the years, they delivered amazing products and services, made their clients very happy, and always had an excellent built-in profit margin. Then something happened. They almost lost their business. I will give you a clue - Mexican Peso, US Dollar, and Euro.

You will also read about how on the second call with a new prospect, he told me, *"You better start looking for a new job because when your company finds out that you're giving their money away, you will be fired."* I had just told this CFO of the new company that I could save him $29,000CAD (Canadian Dollar) on one of the world's simplest currency conversions, converting Canadian Dollars to $2,500,000USD United States Dollars. He wanted to know how I thought I could save him any money when his bank has been doing his conversions at *"MARKET RATE,"* and because he was such a great customer, they did not charge him anything; it was a *"FREE SERVICE."*

If any of this sounds familiar, you're in the right place. I did not write this book for Hedge Fund Managers, Currency Traders, or Stockbrokers. I wrote this book for the same type of people I have been working with for the last 20 years, small to medium-sized businesses who do international business and must deal with multiple currencies.

After reading this book, you will be on a more even playing field with the financial institutions' professionals. Understanding how they trade the Foreign Exchange Market, what terminology they use, and the instrument options you can use to hedge your position; gives you a huge advantage in dealing with this close-knit community.

I have based this book on my 40 years of experience in the financial services industry. For the last 20 years, I have been focused on servicing clients who use the Foreign Exchange Market to hedge their international currency risk. The outline of this book came from a 2-day Workshop I developed and presented at UCLA Extension. I geared the Workshop toward importers/exporters, manufacturers, distributors, small banks, CPAs, and other businesses that use the Foreign Exchange Market as an important part of their financial strategy. These people deal with the issues discussed in this book and suffer the consequences of not understanding how things work in the Foreign Exchange Market's very private world.

Here you will learn the terms they use so you can sound like someone that understands this world. I will show you how the Foreign Exchange Market is different from any other market in the world. The first difference is that it is by far the largest market in the world. Larger than the combined dollars traded per day of all the stock and commodity exchanges combined, over $5.4 trillion traded every day.

You must first understand that everything you do to hedge or convert currency starts with trading. After that, you will learn the 9 different risks associated with the Foreign Exchange Market and the 5 main financial instruments used to hedge these risks.

Delivery or Currency Conversion could be a book by itself. In that Section, I will show you how, in many of the world's largest banks, this is the single most profitable function within the bank. Learning how to take charge of this procedure within your company can change the accounting and treasury department from an expense to a profit center.

I have worked closely with traders on the currency desk of firms I worked for, my clients' traders, and institutional desks. I built close relationships with these traders. And most importantly, I learned how this market works, and that is what I want to share with you.

What you will learn in this book:

- What are the 9 main risk factors when doing business involving foreign currency?
- What are the 5 main currency hedging instruments?
- What are the terms used by the professionals in the Foreign Exchange Market?
    - For example, I grew up on the south side of Chicago. Growing up there, a *buck* was a $1.00 bill. Friends of mine grew up in Wisconsin and thought of a *buck* as a male deer. However, in the worl of Foreign Exchange, a *buck* is $1,000,000. You can see why using the proper term is important.
- How can you figure out if the financial institution is making a huge markup on your transaction?
- What makes the Foreign Exchange Market move?
- How to pick the best instrument for your hedge.

What you will not learn in this book:

- How to become a currency trader
- How to develop a hedging strategy for a huge multi-national company with complex Foreign Exchange positions
- How to take the first price you get for a currency conversion

An Insider's Guide to Currency Hedging and Conversions

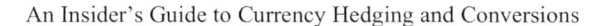

Welcome to the World of Foreign Exchange

This is like nothing you've traded before!

So, you want to start or improve your hedging to lower risk in this area of your business. You might be new to hedging, or you might have dabbled in it and became frustrated, possibly losing a lot of money, and were then too afraid to take that gamble again. Even worse, you might have paid a huge markup without even knowing what the institution built into your *"FREE SERVICE."* The only way to know this is to understand the ground rules and to know the basics of how and why this system can work for you.

When I first started looking into hedging, I thought it was very confusing too. Why would anyone do this when there were other easier ways? When I finally understood these methods, I started to think: "Why would anyone do anything else?"

It is important that you understand the Foreign Exchange Market. We will look at the history of the United States Monetary System and develop an understanding of the terminology used to transact business in this market. Next, we will look at the major types of risk you can face doing business internationally that involve multiple currencies. Once you have a strong understanding of the basics, I will explain how the Foreign Exchange Market trades. This will provide you with a foundation for evaluating the potential hedging instruments. Understanding how these instruments work is necessary to develop strategies that will use the best instrument for the safest results at the lowest cost.

We will examine the 9 Foreign Exchange Risk Factors every company that does business internationally has to deal with. These risk factors are above and beyond the normal risk factors of just doing international business. To mitigate these currency risks, the financial services industry has created several instruments designed to help offset Foreign Exchange Risk. Knowing the risk factors, we will investigate the many different hedging techniques available to most companies. We will take an in-depth look at the 5 most common financial instruments used to hedge foreign exchange risk using real-world examples of how these can benefit or harm your company.

As I will explain later in the book, financial institutions do not want you to know how they offer these "**FREE SERVICES**" and somehow still end up making thousands of dollars on each simple transaction.

I will show you how to avoid being taken advantage of by these institutions that use the *"NO FEE"* sales pitch. They charge you rates that you would never agree to if you understood how much money they really made on servicing your foreign currency needs. I will introduce you to several different ways to hedge your currency risk, as well as how to manage currency conversions at the best possible price - not the price you're quoted. You will also learn how to negotiate the exchange rate and markup of both your hedges and deliveries.

First of all, we will cover the real risk involved in doing business that involves foreign currency. To do this you have to understand how the International Foreign Exchange Market works. Then we will discuss how the professionals trade this market and examine the areas they do not want you to know about. Understanding how the Currency Markets trade is key to the knowledge that you need to evaluate the possible hedges, as well as the actual cost of your currency conversion.

Next, I will provide you with an understanding of potential risks and then all the options you have to hedge those risks. You will learn many ways to protect your profits. Your bank does not charge for several types of transactions, and yet these transactions can cost you thousands of dollars each time you hedge your position or convert currency. The real reason many banks do these transactions for free is that they could never admit to you the outrageous amount of money they make on such a simple transaction. The other issue with the banks doing business like this is that you cannot compare prices or use different strategies to save you money without knowing what they are making.

I was involved with several projects that I explain in **Case Studies** throughout the book; they are short recaps of these types of transactions. I will give you two quick examples of how currency hedging and currency conversion should not be considered a simple clerical job. After you finish this book, you will agree that only senior-level treasury people should be doing this kind of negotiating. It can cost your firm anywhere from thousands of dollars to millions of dollars per year.

The use of **Forward Contracts** is prevalent because they are easy to do, and they **seem** to be free. This example will show how wrong this logic is and how much money this **"free service"** can really cost.

A few years back, I worked with a sizeable multi-company family business in Mexico. I will go into details later, but for now, I will just tell you that I suggested an options strategy. The client insisted on using Forward Contracts, and it cost him $2,700,000 by the time it was all over.

I will also show deals with "*at the market*" currency conversions and how much a free service can actually cost your company. This case study will show how one simple **"FREE"** monthly conversion from the Canadian Dollar to the US Dollar can cost your firm millions over a few years.

Introduction to the InterBank Market

This IS the Foreign Exchange Market

Like I said earlier, the **Foreign Exchange Market** is unlike any other Market in the world. It is nothing like the Stock or Commodity Markets we all trade on. The main difference is that there is:

- **no** centralized Foreign Exchange Floor
- **no** building that acts as an Exchange to trade currencies
- **no** centralized authority
- **no** centralized computer center to track the trades
- **no** centralized clearing facility

What there is that functions as an Exchange is known as the **InterBank Market**.

The InterBank Market is made up of many large money center banks around the world. These banks include:

- the Central Banks of most countries
- large multinational banks
- money center banks
- some smaller banks that make a market in just one or two currencies
- non-bank institutions such as major brokerage firms, hedge funds, and some large corporations

Foreign Exchange Market Today

Where and how the Foreign Exchange Market Trades

The Foreign Exchange Market (InterBank Market) today comprises over 1,000 international banks from around the world. These banks are available to trade currencies between each other, as well as with brokerage trading desks and corporations. These banks trade over $5.4 trillion per day without using an Exchange to normalize trading and guarantee trade settlement.

The InterBank Market is also known as the Foreign Exchange Market, Currency Market, Forex Market, or only as the FX Market.

Although this Market is dominated by the largest banks globally, many others take advantage of their liquidity. These additional players range from central banks to multinational corporations, to governments, to financial institutions, to individual speculators, all with very different reasons for being part of the market.

There are several reasons why this Market is unique in comparison to the other standardized, exchange-traded markets. The most obvious reason is the sheer size of the Market's trading volume. This Market trades 24 hours a day, 5 ½ days a week. The Market opens at 5 pm EST on Sunday and remains open until 4 pm EST on Friday. Also unique to this Market is the variety of traders participating every day.

Without a central exchange, the Market truly is global. For example, a corporation in the United States can trade with a bank in Europe for funds delivery of the Japanese Yen to complete a transaction in Tokyo.

This Market has been called the closest to the perfect market for any investor. With the sheer volume traded, it's impossible for anyone but a central bank to manipulate it.

By far, London is the center of foreign exchange trading globally, accounting for about 34% of the total trading in currencies each day. New York comes in second at about 16%, with Tokyo in third place with 6%.

When doing any large currency transaction, it is crucial to make sure your transaction is timed to the market with the most liquidity for the currencies involved.

The trading times for the three major Markets are expressed in local time below:

London	8:00 AM	4:30 PM
New York	8:30 AM	4:30 PM
Tokyo	8:00 AM	5:30 PM

Three vital economic fundamentals that affect the exchange rate of any currency:

- *Change in interest rates*

    o Rising interest rates = increase in the value of a country's currency

    o Declining interest rates = decrease in the value of a country's currency

- *Change in the inflation rate*

    - Accelerating inflation = appreciating currency rates

    - Decelerating inflation = depreciating currency rates

- *Change in the economy*

    - Strengthening economy = strengthening currency

    - Weakening economy = weakening currency

The History of the U.S. Currency

A trip through the history of the US Dollar and how it got here

You're probably saying right now, a history lesson? If you don't understand precisely how our monetary system was derived, you won't fully understand why we are where we are today, so please humor me and read this. I bet you will learn a few new things and also find them interesting.

1690: *First Colonial Notes*

The Massachusetts Bay Colony was the first of the original colonies to issue paper money.

1775-1791: *U.S. Currency in the Beginning*

To help finance the American Revolution, the Continental Congress authorized printing the new nation's first paper money. Known as "**continentals**," the fiat currency notes were issued in such a large quantity that it led to inflation, which, though mild at first, rapidly accelerated as the war progressed. The notes were backed by the *"anticipation"* of tax revenues. Without solid backing, and since they were easily counterfeited, the notes quickly devalued. Eventually people lost faith in the notes, and the phrase "not worth a continental" came to mean "utterly worthless."

1785: *The Dollar*

In 1785 the Continental Congress determined that the nation's official monetary system would be based on the *DOLLAR*. Although this was agreed to in 1785, the first coin representing the new system would not be minted for several more years.

1791-1811: *First Attempt at Central Banking*

At the urging of Treasury Secretary Alexander Hamilton, Congress established the First Bank of the United States, *Bank of North America*, headquartered in Philadelphia in 1781. It was the largest corporation in the country and was dominated by big banking and money interests. Many agrarian-minded Americans, uncomfortable with the idea of a large and powerful central bank, opposed it. By 1811 when the bank's 20-year charter expired, Congress refused to renew it by one vote.

1791: *First United States Bank Note*

After the Continental Congress adopted the Constitution. Congress then had the right to issue paper banknotes to eliminate confusion and to simplify trade. The bank served as the United States Treasury's fiscal agent, performing the first central bank's duties.

1792: *First United States Monetary System*

The first Federal Monetary System was established with the charter of the United States Mint in Philadelphia. The first United States coins were minted in 1793.

1836-1865: *The Free Banking Era*

State-chartered banks and unchartered "*free banks*" took hold during this period, issuing their own notes, redeemable in gold or spices. The proliferation of banks, 1,600 in 1836, also began offering demand deposits to enhance commerce. With over 30,000 varieties of color and design, State banknotes were easily counterfeited, adding to many bank failures. In response to a rising volume of check transactions, the New York Clearinghouse Association was established in 1853 to provide a way for the city's banks to exchange checks and settle accounts.

1861: *Civil War Demand Notes*

With the United States on the brink of bankruptcy and needing to finance the Civil War, Congress authorized the United States Treasury to issue paper money for the first time in the form of non-interest-bearing Treasury Notes called "***Demand Notes.***"

1862: *The Birth of the Greenback*

The United States Notes replaced Demand Notes. These notes were commonly called *"Greenbacks."* The United States Treasury issued these notes up until 1971. The Secretary of the Treasury was empowered by Congress to have notes engraved and printed. At that time, the printing was done by private banknote companies.

Greenback is now a slang term for United States paper money. Greenbacks got their name from the color of the note. In the mid-1800s the term *"Greenback"* was a negative term because they did not have secure financial backing, and banks were reluctant to give customers the full-face value of the paper money.

1863: *New Design for the Greenback*

The new design for the United States currency incorporated a Treasury seal, line engraving necessary for the difficult-to-counterfeit intaglio printing, intricate geometric lathe work patterns, and distinctive linen paper with embedded red and blue fibers.

1863: *National Banking Act*

During the Civil War, the **National Banking Act of 1863** was passed and provided for nationally chartered banks. These newly nationally charted banks circulated notes that had the backing of United States government securities. An amendment to the Act required taxation on State Bank Notes, but not on National Bank Notes. This taxation accelerated the creation of a uniform currency for the nation. Despite taxation on their notes, state banks continued to flourish due to the growing popularity of demand deposits, which had taken hold during the Free Banking Era.

1865: *Gold Certificates*

The Department of the Treasury issued *"Gold Certificates"* against gold coin bullion deposits and were circulated until 1933.

1866: *National Bank Notes*

The introduction of *"National Bank Notes"* by the United States Treasury was the first currency backed by the United States government securities. These notes became the predominant note very quickly. At that time, 75% of all bank deposits were held in nationally chartered banks. As State Bank Notes were replaced, the value of the United States currency stabilized for a time.

1878: *Silver Certificates*

The Department of the Treasury was authorized to issue *"Silver Certificates"* in exchange for silver dollars. The last issue was in the Series of 1957.

1914: *Creation of the Federal Reserve Bank*

The first United States Dollar was printed in 1914 when the Federal Reserve Bank was established. Within the next 60 years, the United States Dollar became the world's reserve currency.

1920s: *The Beginning of Open Market Operations*

Following World War I, Benjamin Strong, head of the New York Fed from 1914 to his death in 1928, recognized that gold no longer served as the central factor in controlling credit. Strong's aggressive action to stem a recession in 1923, through a large purchase of government securities, gave compelling evidence of the power of open market operations to influence credit availability in the banking system. During the 1920s, the Fed began using open market operations as a monetary policy tool. During his tenure, Strong also elevated the Fed's stature by promoting relations with other Central Banks, especially the Bank of England.

1929: *Standardized Paper Money Design*

Paper money of the day was reduced in size by 25%, and it was standardized with uniform portraits on the face along with emblems and monuments on the back.

1929-1933: *The Market Crash and the Great Depression*

During the 1920s, Virginia Representative Carter Glass warned that stock market speculation would lead to dire consequences. In October of 1929 his predictions seemed to be realized when the stock market crashed, and the Nation fell into the worst depression in its history. From 1930 to 1933, nearly 10,000 banks failed, and by March 1933, newly inaugurated President Franklin Delano Roosevelt declared a bank holiday, while government officials grappled with ways to remedy the Nation's economic woes. Many people blamed the Fed for failing to stem the speculative lending that led to the crash. Some people also argued that an inadequate understanding of monetary economics kept the Fed from pursuing policies that could have lessened the depth of the Depression.

1933: *The Depression's Aftermath*

In reaction to the Great Depression, Congress passed the **Banking Act of 1933, better known as the Glass-Steagall Act** calling for the separation of commercial and investment banking and required the use of government securities as collateral for Federal Reserve notes. The Act also established the **Federal Deposit Insurance Corp. (FDIC),** placed open market operations under the Fed, and required bank holding companies to be examined by the Fed. This practice was to have profound future implications, as holding companies became a prevalent structure for banks over time. As part of the massive reforms taking place, Roosevelt recalled all gold and silver certificates, effectively ending the gold and any other metallic standard.

1935: *Federal Open Market Committee (FOMC)*

The **Banking Act of 1935** called for further changes in the Fed's structure, including creating the Federal Open Market Committee (FOMC) as a separate legal entity, removing the Treasury Secretary and the Comptroller of the Currency from the Fed's governing board. It established a limit of members' terms to 14 years. Following World War II, the **Employment Act** added the goal of promoting maximum employment to the list of the Fed's responsibilities.

1944: *Bretton Woods Agreement*

The **Bretton Woods Agreement** was negotiated in July of 1944 by 730 delegates from 44 Countries at the United Nations Monetary and Financial Conference held in Bretton Woods, New Hampshire, thus giving the agreement the name *"Bretton Woods Agreement."*

Under the Agreement, gold was the basis for the United States Dollar, and other currencies were pegged to the United States Dollar's value. This Agreement came to an end in the early 1970s when President Richard M. Nixon announced that the United States would no longer exchange gold for U.S. currency.

The meeting's goal was to establish an efficient foreign exchange system that would prevent competitive devaluations of currencies and promote international economic growth through expanded international trade.

1945: *Allies pay in gold*

During World War II, the United States supplied the Allied forces, and they paid for the supplies with gold. This led to the United States becoming the largest holder of gold in the world.

1951: *The Treasury Accord*

The Fed largely supported the Treasury's fiscal policy goals from its founding in 1913 to the years up to and following World War II. When the Korean Conflict broke out in 1951, Fed chairman William McChesney Martin again faced pressure from the Treasury to maintain low-interest rates to help provide funds for the new conflict. However, Martin worked closely with the Treasury to break the long-standing practice of supporting government bond interest rates. Since then, the Fed has remained staunchly independent in its use of open market operations to support its monetary policy goals.

1956: *The Fed as a Regulator*

In 1956 the **Bank Holding Company** Act named the Fed as the regulator for bank holding companies owning more than one bank.

1970s-1980s: *Inflation and Disinflation*

The 1970s saw inflation skyrocket as producer and consumer prices rose, oil prices soared, and the federal deficit more than doubled. By August 1979 when Paul Volcker was sworn in as the Fed chairman, drastic action was needed to break inflation's stranglehold on the U.S. economy. Volker's leadership as the Fed chairman during the 1980s, though painful in the short term, was successful overall in bringing double-digit inflation under control.

1972: *The Chicago Mercantile Exchange (CME) introduces Currency Futures*

The CME established currency futures trading on the original seven currencies, and companies flocked to the exchange to hedge currency risk.

1980: *Setting the Stage for Financial Modernization*

The **Monetary Control Act of 1980** required the Fed to price its financial services competitively against private sector providers and establish reserve requirements for all eligible financial institutions. The Act marks the beginning of a period of modern banking industry reforms. Following its passage, interstate banking proliferated, and banks began offering interest-paying accounts and instruments to attract customers from brokerage firms. Barriers to insurance activities, however, proved more difficult to circumvent. Nonetheless, momentum for change was steady, and by 1999 the **Gramm-Leach-Bliley Act** was passed, overturning the **Glass-Steagall Act of 1933.** This Act allowed banks to offer a menu of financial services, including investment banking and insurance sales.

The 1990s: *The Longest Economic Expansion*

Two months after Alan Greenspan took office as the Fed chairman, the Stock Market crashed on October 19, 1987. In response, he ordered the Fed to issue a one-sentence statement before the start of trading on October 20th: "The Federal Reserve, consistent with its responsibilities as the nation's central bank, affirmed today its readiness to serve as a source of liquidity to support the economic and financial system." The 10-year economic expansion of the 1990s came to an end in March of 2001 and was followed by a short, shallow recession ending in November of 2001. In response to the bursting of the 1990s Stock Market Bubble in the early years of the decade, the Fed lowered interest rates rapidly. Throughout the 1990s, the Fed used monetary policy on several occasions, including the credit crunch of the early 1990s, and the Russian default on government bonds to keep potential financial problems from adversely affecting the real economy. The decade was marked by generally declining inflation and the longest peacetime economic expansion in our

Country's history.

September 11, 2001

The effectiveness of the Federal Reserve as a central bank was put to the test on September 11, 2001, as the terrorist attacks in New York, Washington, and Pennsylvania disrupted U.S. financial markets. The Fed issued a one-sentence statement reminiscent of its announcement in 1987. "The Federal Reserve System is open and operating. The discount window is available to meet liquidity needs." In the days that followed, the Fed lowered interest rates and loaned more than $45 billion to financial institutions in order to provide stability to the U.S. economy. By the end of September, Federal Reserve lending had returned to pre-September 11th levels, and a potential liquidity crunch had been averted. The Fed played a pivotal role in dampening the effects of the September 11th attacks on U.S. financial markets.

January 2003: *Discount Window Operation Changes*

In 2003 the Federal Reserve changed its discount window operations to have rates at the window above the prevailing Fed Funds rate and provided rationing of loans to banks through interest rates.

An Insider's Guide to Currency Hedging and Conversions

Foreign Exchange Terminology

Knowing the terminology of this tight-knit community gives you a leg up when negotiating

In this section I have listed some of the most commonly used terms by currency traders and those who deal with the InterBank Market. If you remember most of these terms, then you'll look savvy when talking about currencies.

As with any tight-knit community, currency traders believe they are special even within the trading community. For this reason, just by using the right terminology, the right jargon, you will have a much better chance of getting treated more like a peer than a retail customer.

I thought of just making this a glossary, but no one reads a glossary. You only look there if you're interested enough to know what a word means. I felt it was very important that you at least read the terms over. That way you can make sure that you thoroughly understand where and how to use those particular terms when dealing with your financial institution representative.

If you still have questions, my email is in the About the Author section at the end, just send me an email; I will do my best to help you understand it.

Agent Bank - An agent bank is a bank that provides services on behalf of an entity. An agent bank can offer a wide variety of services for businesses looking to expand internationally. These banks generally act on behalf of another bank or group of banks, but they can act on behalf of a person or business.

Aussie – Slang for the Australian Dollar (AUD)

Base Currency – It is the currency in which an institution maintains its books. The currency being traded and expressed first in a direct quote.

Bid/Ask Price – During regular trading hours, each currency pair always has a bid and an ask available to active traders. The bid price is the price at which a trader is willing to buy, and the ask price is the price at which a trader is willing to sell the pair.

Bids are usually lower than the ask price in a standard market order - clients buy at the ask price, and clients sell at the bid price.

Big Figure – typically refers to the first three digits of an exchange rate that dealers treat as understood in quoting. A EUR/USD Exchange rate of 1.2315. The big figure would be 1.23.

Buck – To an institutional Foreign Exchange Trader, a *Buck* is equal to $1,000,000.

Cable – In the Foreign Exchange Market, the term *Cable* refers to the British Pound/US Dollar BGP/USD. The term's origination is that the transatlantic cable was used to transmit rates between London and New York. *Cable* or *Sterling* can be used for the GBP versus US Dollar exchange rate.

Carry Trade – A carry trade is a trading strategy that involves borrowing at a low-interest rate currency and using those borrowed funds to purchase a currency with a higher interest rate.

Choice Price – This is a term used by institutional currency traders. *Choice Price* happens when the bid price and ask price are the same. The spread in a *Choice Price* quote is equal to zero.

Conversion – This is the process by which one currency is exchanged for a second currency.

Correspondent Bank - Refers to a bank that provides services to another bank - usually in another country. The Correspondent Bank acts as an intermediary or agent for a smaller US Bank. Correspondent Banks are usually used by domestic banks to service transactions that either originate or are completed in foreign countries most often in a foreign currency.

Cross Rates – This is the exchange rate quote for a currency pair where neither one is USD (US Dollar). BGP/CHF quote would be considered a cross rate in the United States, whereas it would be one of the primary currency pairs traded in the UK or Switzerland.

Currency Hedging – This is a transaction strategy used to protect against severe fluctuations in a transaction being done in a foreign currency.

Currency Pair – The two currencies used to make up a currency quote, such as EUR/USD (Euro/US Dollar).

Currency Peg – This is a national policy set by the government at a fixed exchange rate for its currency with a foreign currency or a basket of currencies. By pegging the exchange rate, the currency will stabilize the currency between countries. The currency peg goal is to promote trade, reduce uncertainty, and boost the local income levels.

Currency Risk – Is the risk of incurring losses resulting from an adverse change in the exchange rate.

Delivery – Is the tender and receipt of actual cash currency, the cash payout in a different currency, which results from a currency conversion.

Derivatives – Is a complex investment whose value is derived from the underlying financial asset such as currency. Derivatives may be listed on exchanges or traded in the over-the-counter market. Currency futures and currency options are derivatives.

Euro – This is the currency unit for most EMU countries (Austria, Belgium, Finland, France, Germany, Greece, Ireland, Italy, Luxembourg, The Netherlands, Portugal, and Spain) (EUR).

Eurodollars – Deposits denominated in US Dollars at banks and other financial institutions outside of the United States. Although this name originated because of the large amount of such deposits held at banks in Western Europe, similar deposits in other parts of the world are also called Eurodollars.

Fiat Currency – This currency is a currency established as money by government regulation that is not backed by a commodity such as gold or silver. Fiat currency has value only because the government maintains its value.

Flat – The term *flat* in currency trading is used when a trader wants to sell all his open long positions and buy back all his open short positions. Going *flat* means clearing all your open trades.

Forex – Foreign Exchange – Trading one country's currency for another country's currency.

FX – an abbreviation of Foreign Exchange

InterBank Market – Is a complete network of international private banks and government central banks to trade spot currencies.

Kiwi – Slang for the New Zealand dollar (NZD)

Long Position – A long position happens when you buy a currency pair; if you own the pair, you're *long* the position. For example, being *long* the EUR/USD means you have an open position in the **EUR/USD.**

Loonie – Slang for the Canadian dollar (CAD)

NDF – A Non-Deliverable Forward (NDF) is a currency derivative contract to exchange cash between the NDF and prevailing spot rates. The largest NDF markets are the Chinese Yuan, Indian Rupee, South Korean Won, New Taiwan Dollar, Russian Ruble, and Brazilian Real.

OUT-OF-THE-MARKET – This phrase is commonly used when a broker wants to convince someone that the profit made on a trade came from the market (not that someone lost that amount of money).

Pip – This is the acronym for **Price Interest Point**. It is a tool of measurement related to the smallest incremental move of a currency being quoted. Normally one pip equals 0.0001 for EUR/USD, GBP/USD, USD/CHF, and 0.01 for the USD/JPY.

Pound Sterling – The modern-day base unit of currency for the British Pound (GBP).

Quote Currency – This is the currency used to pay for the transaction. ***Rate of Exchange*** – Usually determined by the natural forces of markets but can be moved by a central bank's intervention.

Risk – The exposure to change, the variability of significantly different returns than those expected.

Risk Management – In the foreign exchange market, the risks that need to be managed include Sovereign, Country, Market, Transfer, Delivery, Credit, and Counterparty Risk. Risk management is developing hedging strategies to offset an unexpected move in any of these possible risks, thereby maintaining profitability in the transaction.

Short – Being *short,* a currency pair means that you have sold a pair you do not own. The reason for selling a pair you do not own is that you believe the pair's value will go down, and you can buy it back at a lower price to flatten your position.

Spot – Is the cash market for the immediate delivery of the currency.

Spread – The spread is the difference between the bid and the ask prices.

Swissy – This is slang for the Swiss Franc (CHF). The abbreviation for the Swiss Franc is derived from Switzerland's Latin name, "Confoederatio Helvetica," with the "F" standing for Franc.

Tick Value – Is the smallest price movement an instrument can move while trading. In the case of Foreign Currencies, the majority of currencies have a Tick Value of 0.00001. For EUR/USD that equals $12.50 per Tick.

Yard – To an institutional Foreign Exchange trader, a Yard equals one billion.

An Insider's Guide to Currency Hedging and Conversions

How the Currency Market Trades

This is how the financial institution you use to hedge or convert currencies looks at the market.

Understanding the Basics

You must clearly understand how the Foreign Exchange Market works if you are going to transact business in other countries. One of the first concepts you must understand is that of **Major Pairs** and **Cross Pairs**.

A Major Pair is any currency paired with the US Dollar. Examples of these are:

Euro Dollar/US Dollar - EUR/USD

British Pound/US Dollar - GBP/USD

US Dollar/Canadian Dollar - USD/CAD

All other pairs are Crosses. These are **non-USD pairs**. Examples of these are:

Euro/Swiss Franc - EUR/CHF

New Zealand Dollar/Japanese Yen - NZD/JPY

One thing you have to always remember is that if you're hedging or converting one currency to another, you're trading

Before we start discussing all the ways we can hedge the many kinds of risk, we need to understand how the International Foreign Exchange Market trades.

We will cover:

- The basics of the International Foreign Exchange Market
- How currencies are quoted to traders and compare those quotes to the ones we receive from our bank or financial institution

When I say that trading currencies is much different from trading other financial instruments, you need to understand why. Not having a centralized trading pricing system means the price you get might not be the best price, just the best price for that group of quote providers.

The first difference is that currencies are quoted in pairs, which means one of the pair's currencies is **Long,** and the other is **Short**. Currency pairs are always quoted the same way - EUR/USD (Euro/US Dollar); it will **never** be quoted USD/EUR.

The first currency in a pair is the **BASE** currency. EUR/USD is a Euro/US Dollar quote with the EUR being the BASE currency.

The second currency in the pair is the **QUOTE** currency. In the EUR/USD, the US Dollar is the QUOTE currency. The BASE currency is always 1 unit, and the QUOTE currency is how much of the QUOTE currency it takes to buy 1 unit of the BASE currency.

Example of EUR/USD Quote from an Institutional Trading Desk

Symbol	BASE	QUOTE
	Bid	Ask
EURUSD	1.18265	1.15266

Spread on this quote = 0.00001 or 1/1,000th of one cent

Quotes like this on institutional platforms, most of the time, have spreads running from "**choice**" where the bid and ask are the same, to a spread of 0.00002 or 2 1/1,000th of a cent.

This is why they say they can do the trade for "*FREE,*" considering most clients only deal with 2-digit cents. Using the example above, if they bought the currency from you at $1.18 and sold it at $1.18265, which is the most straightforward possible trade - requiring no skill and no experience, but merely selling it at the market for a $5,000,000 conversion, the bank would make $13,250 on the spread. Of course, the bank would like to make an even bigger profit, and they sometimes do.

However, making the trade at these rates would only take seconds.

When a EUR/USD unit is purchased, the trader is <u>long</u> the Euro and <u>short</u> the USD. This might seem hard to understand being long and short in the same trade so let me explain. If you were to buy one share of IBM with cash from your trading account, your trade would look like this:

IBM/USD - you are <u>long</u> IBM stock and <u>short</u> US Dollars

Profits or losses are in the QUOTE currency. A loss in a EUR/JPY Euro/Japanese Yen currency pair would be stated in Japanese Yen and then be converted to US Dollars when the trade settles.

Another significant difference between how money is priced in the Currency Markets and how a business looks at the cost of capital is how currencies are priced. The Currency Markets use the term ***"Pip,"*** an acronym for ***"Price Interest Point."*** This is a tool of measurement related to the smallest price movement made by any exchange rate. Currencies are usually quoted in four decimal places, meaning the smallest change in a currency pair would be in the last digit. This would make one pip equal to $1/100^{th}$ of a percent or one Basis Point. This is important when dealing with a financial institution, and you're thinking in cents per dollar, and they are trading in $1/100^{th}$ of a cent or less. In the last few years, much of the trading done in the major currencies are being traded based on a 5th

decimal point - considered 1/10th of that pip or 0.00001.

Exchange rates are carried out to 5 decimal places, EUR/USD 1.26593. The three at the end of the amount is 1/10th of that pip.

Currency Prices

Symbol	Bid	Ask
AUDCAD	0.95170	0.95189
AUDCHF	0.65885	0.65901
AUDJPY	77.250	77.255
AUDUSD	0.72610	0.72620
AUDNZD	1.09313	1.09331
CADCHF	0.69223	0.69241
CADJPY	81.164	81.172
CHFJPY	117.233	117.247
EURAUD	1.62848	1.62871
EURCAD	1.54999	1.55015
EURCHF	1.07315	1.07320
EURGBP	0.89398	0.89406
EURJPY	125.810	125.817
EURNZD	1.78027	1.78059
EURUSD	1.18263	1.18268
GBPAUD	1.82152	1.82182
GBPCAD	1.73371	1.73404
GBPCHF	1.20024	1.20045
GBPJPY	140.719	140.738
GBPNZD	1.99116	1.99177
GBPUSD	1.32283	1.32292
NZDCAD	0.87050	0.87073
NZDCHF	0.60265	0.60283
NZDJPY	70.662	70.670
NZDUSD	0.66420	0.66431
USDCHF	0.90736	0.90746
USDCAD	1.31060	1.31075
USDJPY	106.380	106.385
XAUUSD	1931.1	1931.6

xTasyTrader

The previous chart shows the price quotes for a number of the more common currency pairs. As you can see, the spreads vary, but all are much less than 1 cent. The last quote on the list XAUUSD is the pair for Gold/US Dollar. The XAUUSD trades in $0.10 increments.

The EURUSD quote, Euro/US Dollar, has a spread of:

Bid - 1.18263   Ask – 1.18268

Spread of 0.00005

The AUDCAD quote, Australian Dollar/Canadian Dollar has a spread of:

Bid – 0.95170 Ask – 0.95189

Spread of 0.00019

This quote system is set up for retail forex traders, not institutional traders like the banks and other financial institutions you use for hedging or conversions. With an institutional quote feed, the EURUSD would have a spread of 0.00000 – choice or up to 0.00002.

If you worked with your financial institution to convert $5,000,000 into Euros and bought the Euros at $1.19, which would be a great price for conversion at these prices, the bank would have made $36,600, which is the difference between $1.19 and $1.18268. As I said, this would have been a great deal for you in this market. What if they added a penny to your cost, and you paid $1.20 for the conversion? The financial institution would have made a staggering $86,600! I am sure most of you would not have noticed anything wrong and felt good that your buddy at the bank took such good care of you.

The banks spread would have been tighter, more like choice to 0.00002. For this example, I used the retail feed numbers.

United States Dollar to Euro Conversion Pricing

Purchase Price	$1.20	
Cost	$1.18268	Purchasing the Euro at $1.20
Difference	$0.02	
$5,000,000	$86,600	

Purchase Price	$1.19	
Cost	$1.18268	Purchasing the Euro at $1.19
Difference	$0.00732	
$5,000,000	$36,600	

The AUDCAD quote, Australian Dollar/Canadian Dollar has a spread of:

Bid – 0.95170 Ask – 0.95189

Spread of 0.00019

If you worked with your financial institution to convert $5,000,000CAD into Australian Dollars and bought the Australian Dollars at $.96CAD, which would be a great price for conversion at these prices, the bank would have made $40,550CAD on the difference between $.96 and $.95189CAD. As I mentioned above, this would have been a great deal for you in this market. What if they added a penny to your cost, and you paid $0.97 for the conversion? The financial institution would have made $90,550CAD, and I am sure, just like the previous example, most of you would not have noticed anything wrong and felt good that the bank really cared about you.

As with the EURUSD, this example uses a retail feed. As we know, the institutional feed that banks and other financial institutions use would have a much tighter spread, more like 0.00004 to 0.00008. For this example, I used the retail feed, so the financial institution's real profit would have actually been much larger.

Canadian Dollar to Australian Dollar Conversion Pricing

Purchase Price	$0.96	
Cost	$0.95189	Purchasing the Euro at $0.96
Difference	$0.00811	
$5,000,000	$40,550	

Purchase Price	$0.97	
Cost	$0.95189	Purchasing the Euro at $0.97
Difference	$0.01811	
$5,000,000	$90,550	

The chart above is a EUR/USD (Euro/US Dollar)

4-hour **Candle Chart**

An Insider's Guide to Currency Hedging and Conversions

These 6 Factors Move the Market

Understanding what moves the currency market gives you an advantage when negotiating

How a Nation is viewed by the rest of the World has a lot to do with the power of that Nation's currency. A robust and stable economy coupled with a low threat of war, will also strengthen the currency of that Nation.

1. Interest Rate Differentials

The driving force behind a move in any stable Nation's currency price is their current interest rate. The higher the interest rate, the more traders and corporations holding one currency will exchange it for the higher interest rate currency. This demand for the currency will add to the value of the currency, therefore increasing the exchange rate.

2. Import/Export Activity

The Import/Export business is one of the main reasons this Market exists. Any import/export company's main goal is to sell goods from one country to another country. This action requires exchanging the currency of one country for that of the other country. When the import or export side of a country's trade is out of balance, the results are often reflected in the country's currency exchange rate.

3. Monetary Policy

The Monetary Policy of a nation relates to the demand side of the economic policy. It refers to the actions taken by the country's central bank to control the nation's money supply to meet its financial goals.

4. Economic Fundamentals

Economic Fundamentals include the necessary qualitative and quantitative information that contributes to the financial well-being of the country. These fundamentals are used to set the value of the country's currency concerning all other currencies.

5. Domestic Debt Levels

> The willingness of the private sector to hold debt depends on the risk associated with owning that currency. If a government issues more debt than it can reasonably pay back through taxes and other fees, that government is perceived as an excessively risky investment. It will likely have to pay increasingly higher interest rates.

6. Debt Owed by Foreign Investors in the Local Currency

> A Nation's government issues sovereign Debt in a foreign currency to finance the issuing country's growth and development.

An Insider's Guide to Currency Hedging and Conversions

Why Exchange Rates Change?

This is what it's all about!

There are some theories as to why Foreign Exchange Rates change and some long/short term influences that contribute to these changes:

- *The Asset Theory:*

    When a reliable factor such as real interest rates makes one currency more attractive than others for foreign investors – the currency should appreciate against the other currencies.

- *Supply-and-Demand Theory:*

    When a country sees an increase in its supply of money, prices in that country are expected to rise. When prices rise, consumer demand will decrease, which will likely weaken the currency against the other country's currency.

- *Purchasing Power Parity Theory:*

    If prices increase for products in one country and not in other countries, the first country's currency is expected to lose value against other currencies.

- *Capital Transaction Equilibrium Theory:*

    When trade in one currency increases while it stays even or decreases with other currencies, it is expected to strengthen.

Long Term Influences

- *Balance of Trade:* This is when the demand for one country's products increases the demand for that country's currency over time.

- *Inflation Rate:* Higher inflation rates make one country's currency less attractive because of real value loss.

- *Economic Conditions:* A strong economy will draw investors to that currency and away from currencies of countries that are not as strong.

- *Political Uncertainty:* The more unstable a country is politically, the fewer investors want to keep their money in that country's currency.

Short Term Influences

- *Interest Rates:* As the interest rate of a country's currency increases, investors will more likely want to keep as much of their investment capital in that currency.

- *Relationship Between Currencies:* One currency might increase in value in relation to another currency simply because the other currency has lost strength.

- *Government Intervention:* During times of distress, we see more and more government intervention to prop up a country's currency by injecting large sums of money from the central bank.

Key Indicators that Affect Currencies

These are what the real traders watch

Banks, hedge funds, and savvy investors all consider the currency market as an asset class. The interest rate on the currency is considered the yield on that asset. If a currency is deposited into a bank and the interest rate rises, the demand for that currency will increase, causing that currency's value to increase.

Key Economic Indicators

- *Statement by government officials*
    - When the head of the Federal Reserve of the US Central Bank makes a statement, he can cause the US Dollar to move as much as 5% with just a few words.
    - Usually, it takes the US Dollar 3 months or more to move 5%.

- *Central Bank interest rate announcements*
    - The market builds in the expected move in interest rates before the announcement. If the Central Bank does not change the interest rate for some reason, the results can include a sharp move in the underlying currency.
    - When the Central Bank has an unexpected change to the interest rate, the difference can cause the currency to make a huge move.

- *Minutes of the Central Bank interest rate meetings*
    - After the meeting, at a prescheduled time, they announce whether or not they will change the interest rate. Major currency traders decipher these announcements with the use of keywords triggering huge trading in minutes.

- o The currency market gives its opinion of what they expected before the announcement. If the announcement does not follow the market's widely held belief for some reason, you will see significant moves in the affected currencies within minutes.

- *Central Banks have mandates to control inflation*
  - o All Central Banks in major industrial countries have a similar mandate to keep inflation low and stable over the medium term.
  - o Each Central Bank has a monetary policy that is sensitive to the level of inflation.
  - o To protect your company's currency assets, you should first look at the inflation rate to analyze the likely direction of interest rates and the currency.

- *Consumer Price Index (CPI)*
  - o The CPI is the primary inflation indicator that has been the most consistent for driving currencies higher on a higher-than-expected inflation number and lower on a lower than expected inflation number.
  - o The Central Bank, hedge funds, banks, and savvy traders have keyed in on the core CPI.

- *Personal Consumption Expenditures (PCE) – Import Prices*
    - o If the price of imported goods and services purchased from other countries is rising faster than expected, that means inflation is growing more quickly than expected.
    - o The market will buy the currency in anticipation of higher interest rates.
    - o If the price of imported goods and services is falling, traders will sell the currency.

- *Producer Price Index (PPI)*
    - o This index gives the trader a look at the price movements in the components that will affect product prices in a few months. And this index can be viewed as a critical signal to the future movement in inflation before it happens.

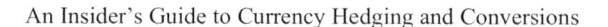

Interest Rates and the Effect on Their Currencies

Interest Rates are the key

Traditionally, a higher interest rate in a country increases the value of that country's currency compared to nations offering lower interest rates. The truth is this simple straight-line calculation rarely exists in the foreign exchange market.

Interest rates can be a major factor in influencing currency value and exchange rates. The final determination of a currency's exchange rate with other currencies results from many interrelated elements that reflect the country's overall financial condition for other nations.

The value of a currency is not determined by interest rates alone. Two other major factors influence the value of a currency. These major influences are political and economic stability and the level of demand for the country's goods and services. These factors are often more important at establishing the value of a country's currency value. With some currencies, the country's balance of trade between imports and exports can be a crucial factor.

The gross domestic product (GDP) is also a key factor in establishing the country's currency value. Also the nation's debt level plays a major role in determining the currency's value.

Global Interest Rates
as of November 2020

Currency	*Interest Rate*
New Zealand Dollar	0.250%
Australian Dollar	0.250%
Canadian Dollar	0.250%
British Pound	0.100%
U.S. Dollar	0.250%
Japanese Yen	0.100%
Euro	0.000%
Swiss Franc	-0.750%

An Insider's Guide to Currency Hedging and Conversions

The Role of the US Dollar

Reserve Currency of the World

The US Dollar (USD) is still the favorite reserve currency of the world. The US Dollar is the most commonly used currency to price and pay for commodities worldwide. As for trading the US Dollar, it is by far the most actively traded currency when combined with other currencies, and the Euro/US Dollar EUR/USD is the most actively traded pair. The only way to convert some less popular currencies to another currency is first to convert the less popular currency to the US Dollar, and then convert the US Dollar position to the new currency.

During World War II, the United States supplied the Allied Forces, and they paid the United States back in gold. From this point the United States became the largest holder of gold in the world. It also led the United States to back its currency with gold or the gold standard. The gold standard was ended by President Richard Nixon. However, the United States remained the favorite reserve currency, with more than 61% of all foreign bank reserves denominated in the United States Dollar. Nearly 40% of the world's debt is in US dollars.

Risk or Exposure

The Difference between Risk and Exposure

Risk refers to the probability that a company will experience losses due to its own decisions.

Exposure refers to the possibility that a company will experience losses due to outside influences.

"Therefore, risk is a result of the company's exposure."

Horcher, K (2005)

This change can adversely affect the anticipated income from a transaction by lowering the conversion rate. A change in the rate can also adversely affect the cost of goods priced in other currencies by increasing the number of US Dollars needed at the time of payment.

The 9 Common Foreign Exchange Risks

Do you even know about half of them?

The variety of potential risky issues involving currency in multinational transactions makes it difficult for an organization to control all aspects of risk, especially when they participate in more than one country's market. The following are the most common forms of currency risk that should be weighed into each decision that involves business transactions involving foreign currencies.

1. **Acceptable Risk**

    Before looking at any of the individual risk factors, you must calculate your Acceptable Risk exposure. There is always a cost associated with hedging, and it is essential first to calculate how much of a loss you are willing to assume before spending any money. After that is in place, you have to decide how much you are willing to pay concerning the amount of potential loss. Different types of hedges will have different risk levels, along with various costs or even cost structures. Knowing your acceptable level of risk first is key to developing the right hedge in relation to the known risk.

2. *Counterparty Risk*

This Risk is based on the creditworthiness of the counterparty country. These agreements require daily balancing and, when needed, increases to the daily margin requirement. As with any transaction using credit as the initial form of payment, the risk assumed is directly related to the other party's ability to meet its required payment needs when due.

The change in daily margin requirements by major financial institutions lately has been unprecedented, with margin requirements on some currencies going from 1% to over 5% within a month. Over time some of these margin rates have exceeded 15%. These changes in the margin requirement can lead to defaults on trades that have already been made. This then leaves the other side of the trade exposed to a shortfall in the currency traded.

These types of changes in the interest rates have become the most critical risk factor for financial institutions.

Varying degrees of Counterparty Risk exists in all financial transactions. In a currency transaction, the counterparty risk is related to the risk that the financial institution you are dealing with will not be able to meet the required payment to settle the currency conversion transaction. This is an average risk for most currency transactions, but with longer-term currency transactions, there can be an additional risk due to the amount of time needed to settle the transaction.

If you are hedging your currency risk to cover a contract that will be completed in 3 years, the additional time adds another layer of risk to the transaction. If the counterparty to the trade becomes insolvent during those three years, you lose your protection and also what you invested in by establishing the hedge.

3. *Market-Liquidity Risk*

This risk is unique to the Foreign Exchange Market. Because this Market trades through the InterBank network, there is no exchange for guaranteeing any of the standard protections you assume when trading an exchange-traded instrument. One of the main reasons Exchanges started was to provide liquidity, even in challenging market conditions. Floor traders offered liquidity to markets and guaranteed that every quote was backed by someone who would take the other side. In the currency market, major banks provide the liquidity for trades with smaller banks as well as trading firms, providing liquidity for smaller trades. Another important difference between the InterBank Market and Exchanges is that the same bank providing liquidity also holds large positions in many of the traded currencies. The

Market-Liquidity Risk comes into play when a currency has a major move, and all the liquidity providers pull back. At these times, there is no one to take the other side of the trade based on the quote. The market will then free fall until the new price is low enough for the major banks to be once again willing to become buyers of the falling currency.

The main reason for a loss of liquidity in the Foreign Exchange Market is when a significant financial institution pulls back from the market, or one of the currencies becomes involved in a national situation that either temporarily or permanently stops the currency from trading freely.

When a company does all its currency-related business exclusively with one financial institution, a problem like this can become a catastrophe for the company. Even if the Foreign Exchange Market as a whole is acceptable, including trading in the currencies in question, if the company's financial institution moves away from the currency for any reason, the position can be at risk.

The loss of liquidity either from the entire Foreign Exchange Market or from a single exclusive financial institution will, at the very least, widen the spreads. Even if one major financial institution moves away from a single currency, the rest of the financial institutions become less aggressive with their pricing, which causes the spreads on that currency to widen. This increases the cost to buy that currency, and less will be received for the same currency if the company is selling the currency back to the institution.

4. *Transaction Risk*

All multinational companies have Transaction Risk. The most common form of risk is a company that sells a product in a foreign currency on credit. The payment for the product is made 60 to 90 days later or longer. This risk happens when the payment is made, and the currency in question has devalued. This will cause the company to receive less than expected in their home currency either when converted or just as a reporting issue.

Overseas projects are often required to submit bids in the local currency. Also, the bids are required to have an exchange rate embedded in the bid. There is a risk that the exchange rate can change before the bid is accepted. This can be dealt with in 2 ways:

- The first is to insert a currency adjustment clause in the contract.

- The second is to develop an option strategy that will cover the move in the currency.

5. *Country Risk*

Country Risk comes from the possibility of exposure to Currency Risk due to changes in a country's economic or political changes. These types of risks range from political elections to natural disasters.

6. *Price Risk*

    This Risk is the exposure to a loss from the change in the value of a commodity or financial instrument. This can happen because of the difference in the exchange rate of the two currencies.

Case Study:

A Canadian company that purchased a US Oil Futures contract and paid for the contract with US Dollars. Over time the company had two risks instead of the usual one. The usual one is the Market Risk of the futures movement. The second additional risk is the value of the US Dollar compared to the value of the Canadian Dollar. Suppose the Canadian Dollar had fallen in value related to the US Dollar, and the price of the futures had moved up. In that case, the company could still have lost money if the futures contract had increased in value and did not cover the loss in the Canadian Dollar.

7. *Credit Risk*

    A company has the same Credit Risk level with an international client that they have with US clients. The company also has an additional risk coming from the carrying cost of debt in the other currency. Interest rates and exchange rates can change during the time the loan is open, causing a loss of expected interest revenue.

8. *Interest Rate Risk*

    This Risk is from changes in the market interest rates of either currency. This Risk can cause paying more in interest charges from the borrowed funds that the company needed or from receiving less interest income from deposits.

Interest Rate Risk can also arise from borrowing or investing in a foreign currency. The change in the local market interest rate will affect the local currency's value relating to other currencies.

9. *International Foreign Exchange Risk*

This Risk is the most common risk when dealing in the Foreign Exchange Market. An adverse change in the exchange rate of one currency can affect a company in any of the following ways:

- Reducing the net cash income
- Increasing the amount of cash needed to meet a current obligation
- Reducing the net reported profit
- Reducing the value of foreign assets
- Increasing the value of its current liabilities in the country

Fluctuations in the Foreign Exchange rates of the currencies involved in a transaction can have the following effects:

- A rate change can adversely affect the anticipated income from a transaction by lowering the conversion rate.
- A change in the exchange rate can also adversely affect the project's profit by changing the cost of goods priced in other currencies by increasing the number of dollars needed at the payment time.

Case Study:

In 1987 there was a sharp fall in the value of the US Dollar. French wine producers chose to maintain their prices in Francs for export to the US. As a consequence, the US consumers switched to the less expensive California wines. This also led to more exports from the US to Europe and the California wine industry's strong growth. These events greatly reduced the demand for French wines.

Strategies for Managing Currency Risk

The inexact science of Managing Foreign Exchange Risk

To diversify a currency portfolio, companies seek out asset classes whose returns are negatively correlated. Therefore, if the returns on one asset class go down, the returns on the other asset class(es) have a propensity to go up.

The markets themselves have created financial management tools to help companies hedge their exposure to risk while not diversifying their transactions into other asset classes.

Remember that Risk Management Strategies are not binary decisions. They can (and often ought to) be modified while the transaction is exposed to potential risk.

Continuous Hedging Decisions

- ✓ Continue to monitor potential risk for the transaction
- ✓ Modify Risk Management Strategies as needed
- ✓ Three options that a company has when presented with a situation that might need to be hedged:

    - **Don't hedge anything.**

    - **Hedge everything.**

    - **Hedge some of the exposure, but not all of it.**

Developing a Risk Management Program

Systemizing Currency Risk Management

As we all know, risk is inevitable in any business transaction. Success or failure depends mainly on how well the company's management anticipates the risks and develops plans to deal with those risks. This section will deal with only the additional risk faced by multinational companies due to the additional risk of multiple currency transactions. Each of the typical financial risks takes on an extra level of complexity because of the continually changing Foreign Exchange Market.

One of the potential benefits of doing business in multiple currencies is that the currencies involved could move in the company's favor. The idea is to take advantage of these moves, and when possible, use the movement to increase profits. This can be done simply by moving excess cash from other currencies that are either losing in the currency market or staying relatively stagnant. This is the simplest way of profiting from a positive move in a currency.

Currencies tend to move in one direction for a more extended period than, say, stocks. Considering how much money it takes to change the direction of a currency, it is often safe to assume that if the currency moves in the company's favor, it will continue in that direction for a while. If the company treats its currency as a trading asset, you have to treat it like one. Be vigilant to the currency's signs of stopping its move or even changing direction. Even if you only consider it as a cash asset, you still need to monitor the return on that asset in relation to the return on other currencies.

Similarly, a company can benefit from a currency move in its favor. A movement against the currency will cost the company real money. Companies must remember that all the currencies it owns are an asset and must be monitored like any other asset. It is easy to ignore the loss in a currency move because it does not show up on any statement or report. Only by consistent monitoring of each currency will the company be able to maximize its profit through the use of foreign currency, or at least limit the losses due to a change in either the foreign exchange rate or interest rate.

Case Study:

When I became the CFO of a public company in the financial services industry, I studied our international office and international clients who paid in foreign currency. I wanted to see how well we had managed this asset. In the previous year, I found out that the company did not control the foreign currencies it dealt with, and by doing so, lost just over $50,000. The loss was caused by not negotiating the better exchange rates for conversions to US Dollars. **(*The vital thing is that this loss never showed up on any report or any statement*).** The conversions were done at *"Market Rate"* by large, respected financial institutions. Only because of my prior experience in the Foreign Exchange Market was I able to verify that the exchange rates were much too broad.

Companies involved in business transactions such as commodities, raw materials, shipping, and power are affected by each of these price movements. International companies must deal not only with the cost of the product but also the effect that the conversion rate (from their currency to the currency that the product is priced in) will affect the actual price of the product. These firms usually have a hedging or risk operation to follow the product's cost and establish hedges to protect the company against moves that could cause significant losses. Some, but not all by far, also include currencies in their hedging programs.

A good example of this is when a Canadian oil company has its operating cost in Canadian Dollars (CAD), but oil is traded in US Dollars (USD). If oil prices remain constant in USD, but the USD weakens against the CAD, the company's revenue will decrease, while its operating cost remains the same.

An Insider's Guide to Currency Hedging and Conversions

Evaluating Risk before Entering a New Market

Before you enter that exciting new international market, make sure you know the Foreign Exchange Risk

It is crucial to evaluate the Foreign Exchange Risk when entering a new market. A company's Foreign Exchange Risk Plan is often overlooked.

I have shown below a sample checklist that should be part of every Expansion Plan.

- ✓ Is the currency used considered a major market or an emerging market currency?

- ✓ Is it a freely traded currency with both purchases and sales permitted?

- ✓ Does the currency exchange rate operate under a pegged or target rate regime?

- ✓ Can funds be freely moved into as well as out of the country?

- ✓ Are forwards, options, and the other hedging instruments available for hedging?

- ✓ Can the business be transacted in a major currency such as USD or EUR, as well as the local currency?

- ✓ Can local banks handle both local and international currencies?

- ✓ Can the company open different currency accounts at the same bank?

- ✓ What is the underlining legal system?

- ✓ What are the limitations on currency transactions?

Understanding Hedging?

"Hedging is the business of seeking assets or events that offset or have a weak or negative correlation to an organization's financial exposures."

(Horcher, 2005)

We All Hedge Risk When We buy insurance against:

- Loss of property (Hedge against property loss)
- Business interruption (Hedge against unknown events that can stop or severely slow down your business)
- Health Insurance (Hedge against medical bills)
- Car Insurance (Hedge against damage to your car or another car from an accident)

Currency Hedging

Currency hedging is a strategy used by companies to help prevent potential losses on their international business transactions. This requires the use of multiple currencies when the exchange rates move in an unanticipated direction for any of the currencies involved. So, hedging is simply a way of protecting an investment from the potential risk inherent with carrying exposure to the volatility of exchange rates for tradable currencies.

For example, suppose a U.S. company has a contract for services that is being paid to a branch office in Germany in six months. In that case, the company may want to hedge the value of its contract there against a possible weakening of the USD against the EUR. To hedge against that scenario, the company might sell the USD and buy the EUR. This way, if the EUR strengthens against the USD, this contract will be worth more, and they will not have to spend more USD for the same services. The downside might seem to be that if the EUR's value against the USD weakens, their hedge loses its value. However, if the EUR weakens against the USD, they will choose to either get out of their position at a loss or stay in the position until the next favorable market move. This will give the opportunity to sell and pay for the services with dollars worth more than when the contract was signed. If the company does not have enough capital to stay in its contract and needs to get out of it to pay for the services, the hedge has at least acted like insurance. This type of long-term position is called a "Carry Trade."

There are several other options that the company can employ as a hedge against losses in their currency position. For this example, the simplest of these is what a company might do when moving to another country – the company could open a bank account in the country where they would be residing and wire money from the U.S. account to the new account. The possible disadvantage with this method is the exorbitant exchange rates that banks charge their customers and the low-interest rates they offer. The company could also buy a Forward Contract on the currency they will need at the end of six months. The problem with Forward Contracts is that not only do they have high exchange rates, but the company would also have to pay broker commissions.

Moreover, Forward Contracts are always fixed to a certain date. Should the company need the money they put down for the Forward Contract, the company will be penalized for early termination of the Contract. With a Futures Contract, the company would not have the money locked-up as they would with a Forward Contract. Still, they would also have to pay the spread in addition to the broker's commission, and it would not be able to choose the exact amount of USD the company would like to convert to another currency since Futures Contracts are exchanged in fixed lots. A EUR to USD contract is sold in lots of $125,000, whereas GBP to USD contracts are sold in lots of $62,500. Another possibility for the company would be to use Currency Options (or FX Options). Generally speaking, corporations prefer to hedge transactions that will definitely happen on a future date with forward contracts. For transactions that may or may not happen on or before a future date, they prefer to hedge their risk with options. Just like other commodities options, the trader has the right but not the obligation to convert one currency into another at a set exchange rate on a specific date in the future. However, the downside of Currency Options, like with the other methods, are the costs involved with Currency Options. They, too, have fixed lot sizes and fixed face values, but in addition to those costs are the premiums that would have to be paid by the investor and the hedge differential. Yet, they do not have the potential for unlimited losses like Forward Contracts.

Understanding the differences in these different types of currency hedges gives the company the ability to develop a custom hedge that will protect the company at the best price.

Why should Companies Hedge Risk?

There is no reason for a company to hedge any risk as long as everything goes their way

There is no reason for you to hedge any risk as long as everything goes your way. However, in the real-world things seldom go your way. Knowing that, keep the following points in mind.

- Foreign Exchange hedging can significantly reduce or even eliminate risk exposure to long-term transactions.
- Hedging provides a way of ensuring that the revenue received, or the cost of goods purchased, will be predictable.
- In a proper hedge, the company can know the maximum profitability range without concern for what the currency markets do.
- Small companies can reduce the uncertainty of changing exchange rates by working with suppliers who quote in the local currency; the supplier takes on the risks involved with exchange rate fluctuations.

Currency Hedging is Hedging, right?

I want you always to remember that a hedge in any market is not a money-making strategy. Let me state that again: **A Hedge in any market is not a money-making strategy**. A currency hedge is meant to protect the company from losses, not to make a profit.

The second part to remember is that most hedges are intended to remove only a portion of the exposure risk rather than all of it. The reason for removing only a part of the risk is the cost associated with the hedge can outweigh the benefits after a certain point.

For example, let's say a German company sells equipment to a US company in US Dollars. The German company can protect a portion of the transaction by buying a currency option to protect the company if the Euro increases in value against the US Dollar. If the company is unprotected and the US Dollar strengthens or stays stable against the Euro, then the company is only out the option's cost.

An Insider's Guide to Currency Hedging and Conversions

Developing Your Hedging Strategy

You need a Hedging Strategy; you might need more than one

When you set out to develop your company's Foreign Exchange Hedging Strategy, you will first have to define your company's risk tolerance. The company needs to set limits on both the level of loss they are willing to take on this deal and also how much they are willing to spend to make sure that no matter what, these limits are never exceeded. In a large company, this is often part of the Treasury Departments Risk Management Guidelines. In a smaller firm, this is usually up to the senior management team or the owner. No one wants to think about losses when they enter into a new and exciting deal, but this is when it must be done. Once the strategy is in place, the instruments are purchased, and the hedge is on, everyone can go back to being proud of themselves for locking in the new deal.

As you have learned earlier in this book, there are many different currency risk factors and several different types of financial instruments that you can use to offset risk. Choosing the right instrument or set of instruments is key to establishing a successful strategy.

The first step in creating any hedge is to consider all of the inherent and extenuating risk factors. Once you have a clear understanding of all of the potential risks, you can start looking at the different financial instruments offered to protect against these risks. Selecting the right instrument or instruments is the key to the success of the hedge. After you have selected the hedging structure, you need to shop the transaction to find the best possible price for the right instrument.

If you're doing any form of hedging now or thinking about starting, it's a good time to work with a professional who understands all of the choices outlined in this book. You want to make sure that you're not overpaying for your hedge, but you also want to be sure you're covered no matter what happens.

> *You have to remember that every time you put a hedge on that, it's different. Even if it's the same currency, for the same amount, and the same length of time, the world is different, the markets are different, and you have to make sure that you have the right protection you need from the start.*

The strategy that you use will be based on where the Foreign Exchange Market is at that time, as well as where the market is forecasted to be by the end of the hedge. Based on your risk assessment, you will need to develop a tactical strategy to ensure all of the known risks are covered and that the cost of this coverage is within your company's guidelines. It is not uncommon for a hedging strategy to have multiple instruments to meet all the hedge requirements. For example, you might use a Spot Purchase because you believe the currency involved will move higher in relation to the dollar over the short term. You might also use a Collar Strategy to cover the overall timeframe of the hedge. These more complex strategies provide several levels of protection.

Working with a professional to help develop this strategy is often the least expensive way to create the right hedge for your situation. It is important to find someone who is not part of an institution with a certain financial instrument to sell.

You might have a great relationship with your banker, but then again, he wants you to use his products and services. As we discussed earlier, much of your hedge's development is based on the negotiated prices you or your consultant have arranged after getting quotes from several financial institutions. Once you have created several successful hedging strategies, you will know the financial institutions that want to work with you and that will provide the products and services you need to meet your goals at the best possible price.

You have to remember that there is something strange with getting a "**FREE**" service when the firm providing that service makes 10's of thousands of dollars on that transaction. It might be "**FREE**" to you, but shouldn't you share in the transaction's profit? To find out how "**FREE**" your transaction really is, be sure to look at the numbers for exiting the position; many of these transactions are "**FREE**" to enter but have a built-in profit for the institution at the end. There are many moving parts in all of these types of transactions and even more ways to structure each of them. Your job is to provide the best coverage and limit your financial risk at the best possible price.

Using the right structure and the right instruments at the right cost to implement your strategy will minimize the risk. This will then protect your company's profits from losses caused by unexpected situations within this volatile market.

Once the hedge is in place, your responsibility will move from creating the hedge to monitoring it. Markets change, sometimes in your favor, sometimes against you. Still, depending on the financial instrument you used, a positive move in the Foreign Exchange Market regarding the exchange rate might be very expensive to your company if you keep the hedge in place. Refining the hedge is common and not to be considered a poor strategy. It can just happen in a market that has the potential to move as quickly as the Foreign Exchange Market.

If caught in time, small changes to the strategy will be inexpensive and give better long-term protection. If left as is, the results can become very expensive for protection that is no longer needed. This is not an insurance policy you buy and forget it. It's an investment that needs to be monitored regularly to maintain that constant level of protection.

Always Remember

You Hedge in your Hedging Account

You Trade in your Trading Account

As you monitor your hedge position, you will be watching the currency market price movement. After some time, you will most likely start reading the market and believe that you can make money trading currencies, as well as hedging with your new-found knowledge. That is fine, that is actually very common, but it has nothing to do with your hedging; **leave your hedge alone!**

I have seen people take their hedging account and start trading the hedge positions. Most of the time, they lose on the trade, and then they have to pay even more to replace the hedge.

If you want to trade the currency market fine, open a trading account, **but leave your hedge alone**. You can open a trading account either for the business or for your personal use. It all depends on where the money comes from for the trading account and where you want the profits or losses to go.

If you open a trading account for the company, make sure you not only check with your broker but also with your attorney to verify your company can have such an account and that the board has authorized you to trade the account. Most likely, you will have to have the board sign off on this as well as the senior management team. If you're the owner, you can do what you want but still, talk to your attorney and tax accountant about where the money should come from before you start trading.

5 Hedging Instruments

Did you even know that you could use a zero-cost collar to hedge?

In an attempt to hedge organizations' currency risks when participating in financial transactions, the Markets have created various tools and strategies to lessen the potential loss from possible adverse market conditions.

The most complex type of hedging instrument falls under the category of Derivatives Securities. These types of instruments are typically used by governmental agencies, banks, financial institutions, asset management firms, and corporations doing business internationally to manage risk. It is essential for executives of firms that do business internationally to have a general knowledge of how these products work and the benefits each brings to the table regarding financial risk management. Understanding each of these instruments gives the executive what he needs to intelligently discuss these options with investment professionals.

The instruments are used when trading: currencies, commodities, stocks, interest rates, fixed income securities, credit, weather futures, etc.

Now that you understand the risks involved, let's start learning which instruments are available and how to select the best one for your specific hedging requirement.

The following chapters will include:

Spot Market

Forward Contracts

Foreign Exchange Futures

Foreign Exchange Swaps

Foreign Exchange Options

Spot Market

Hedging with cash sometimes is the best hedge

The **InterBank Exchange Rate** is the current rate at which Currency Pairs are bought and sold. Remembering that there is no centralized exchange or clearing operation, the exchange rate quoted could be much different from the exchange rate traded between InterBank members or other financial institutions in general. The true Spot Market always quotes one currency vs. another - EUR/USD is the price that it costs in US Dollars for one Euro.

The difference between a Spot Market Price and a Forward Contract Price is that the Spot Market Price is the price <u>now</u> rather than the currency's price in the <u>future</u>.

Spot Market Pricing

- This is the InterBank rate that these currencies are currently trading at for delivery.

- This is the rate that is used to calculate all other rates for Forwards, Swaps, and Options.

- Spot trades are the most common form of speculative trading in the FX Market.

- Banks say they will do a currency conversion at no fee. That they will do it *"at the market price."* Customers believe that the price is the same as the spot rate - it's usually not - it's at the market price set by the bank's risk manager.

- Currency trades for immediate value date traditionally require two banking days for settlement. The settlement date is known as the spot value date because that is the date the funds are delivered with good value to the counterparties' bank accounts.

During these two days, the following activities must take place:

- ✓ Verification of the transaction through an exchange of confirmations between the counterparties.

- ✓ The issue of settlement instructions by each counterparty to its bank to pay the contracted amount on the appointed date.

- ✓ Satisfying exchange control requirements where these exist.

These are some of the *exceptions* to the two-day settlement rule:

- ✓ A transaction for USD against the Canadian Dollar (CAD) is usually delivered and settled on the next banking day.

- ✓ Foreign currency markets in the Middle East are closed on Friday but open on Saturday. A transaction involving the USD exchange for Saudi Riyals could have a split settlement date - the USD being delivered for settlement on Friday and the Saudi Riyals being delivered for settlement on Saturday.

Case Study:

I worked with a very successful Mexican company that was in the marble installation business. The company was generations old and, over time, had become one of the premier marble installation companies for major hotels in Mexico, Canada, and the United States. The company was accustomed to signing contracts sometimes years before the marble was to be installed. As part of their work, the company was in charge of obtaining the marble, customizing the marble to sizes set by the designer, transporting the marble to the site, and then installing it.

As I mentioned before, this company had been doing this work for decades. The family had grown wealthy from their hard work. They never believed in using credit for any part of their projects and never hedged any currency risk.

After their first year of losing money in many decades, they decided to see what ideas we had to help them prevent this in the future. They explained that the previous year was one of the best years in the company's history. They had record sales, record installations, and pleased customers that always paid on time. Their markups on the marble and labor costs were the same as before, and they never had a problem maintaining their expected profit margins.

We went over their spreadsheets for the previous year, and it was apparent what had happened. As I mentioned before, they usually signed contracts years in advance of purchasing the marble, doing the fabrication, and then the installation. Over the previous year, the currency markets had made some significant moves that greatly affected their real bottom line.

To understand their problem, let me explain the currencies involved. The company is headquartered in Mexico and does all the large fabrication in Mexico. They have a massive operation with a sizable workforce at the plant. All of these expenses, as well as the labor costs, were paid out in Mexican Pesos. Their onsite installers were also Mexicans, and they were paid in Pesos even if they were working in Canada or the United States.

The marble purchased by the company for their clients was always bought from a large marble company in Italy. They worked with this firm for decades and had always received great pricing and an excellent product. The firm in Italy was always paid in Euros.

The last part of the equation was the contract itself; it was a contract written for a US Hotel chain and priced in USD. Previously this had always been fine, and they never ran into a problem because of the exchange rate.

The problem was that during the previous year, when the labor cost was the highest on this project, the Mexican Peso had increased in value to the United States Dollar. This meant that it took more US Dollars to cover their labor cost than they had initially planned. The plant cost and corporate overhead also took more US Dollars to cover the same value.

The Euro also strengthened against the US Dollar, so the marble's real cost was much higher than they planned. Also, the shipping cost of marble to the United States was paid in Euros.

At the time they signed the deal, everything looked great. This should have been very profitable. However, moves in the Foreign Exchange market took all their profits and money out of their pockets. Only because it was such a great family business and since the family had saved a large sum of cash in case something unforeseen ever happened, could they meet their obligations to their vendors, as well as to their employees, and remain in business.

The fix going forward was easy. They needed to take their project schedule and add currency hedges to ensure they could meet all their expenses and keep the profit margin they planned for now over the next few years until the contract was completed.

Currently using hedges, they no longer have to worry about losing their family business because of a major move in the Foreign Exchange Market.

This case was very personal to me since it was a multi-generational family business. Still, any time you can get people to understand how to use these tools, it is very gratifying.

Negotiating:

The Spot Currency Market is designed for negotiations. No trading floor, no exchange, no central clearing, thousands of liquidity providers, but when it comes down to buying another currency and taking delivery, you're really doing one transaction with one other firm.

I always enjoyed watching the traders on our currency desk search for the best deal. These traders had years of experience working at central banks and financial institutions doing nothing but trading currencies. I saw multiple traders work the phones for hours to get the best possible deal for a large client. They had the most sophisticated trading systems on their desks, but they went to their phones when they did not see the numbers they wanted. These traders knew the traders at most of the big trading desks in the United States and combined, they knew most of the traders internationally in those focused markets. This is where I learned how to negotiate spot currency deals.

Many key issues direct the negotiations. The currency involved is a big part of it. A large portion of our trading was in Mexican Pesos, so over time, all of the desks in both the US and Mexico knew that if they had a large position in Pesos to sell, that we could possibly be the buyer. This took us to the place where, when an institution had to sell a large number of Pesos, they would call our desk in the morning and say – "Please call us first; we will beat any price in the market since we are dumping Pesos." Unless your firm does mountains of currency deliveries, you will not get these calls, but what you want to do is to have relationships with firms with active trading desks and look for those specializing in the currencies you need to trade.

The second key issue is size - **trust me on this - size does matter!** Even if you only do a few large transactions a year, the size will get desks you talk to excited. If the size is there and it is not a EUR/USD or CAD/USD, you should contact at least five currency trading desks. The more exotic the currency, the wider the spread will be between desks. Some desks will just throw a number out there, and if you take it, great, they make a lot of money. Others will really try and work the trade with at least one coming up with a good price. Over time you will learn which desks are best to call for different currencies and which desks to call for different sizes.

Developing these desk contacts will not be easy; every institution protects traders like walking gold bars. You will have to find someone that can get you through their existing connections, and after time you will be able to handle all of this on your own.

When you have a big trade, you should be able to shop it around to 3 to 6 desks and see who has the best price.

I would also suggest signing up for a good online currency trading platform. Not that you will be doing any trading, at least not at first, but you will be able to see the market. You will most likely be looking at a retail feed with retail prices, but they are a good starting point. You will know that the prices you get from the desk should be better, or even much better, than the spreads you're looking at on the quote system.

An Insider's Guide to Currency Hedging and Conversions

Forward Contracts

Banks love to have you use these to hedge; why?

One of the oldest investment Derivatives for hedging currency risk is the Forward Contract. The Forward Contract serves as the basis for many other types of derivatives used in currency hedging today.

A Forward Contract is a customized derivative contract that obligates one party to buy (receive) and the other party to sell (deliver) an asset at a specified price on a future date. For this discussion, the asset is cash in another currency. Although this might sound like an Option Contract and is often entered into with the purchaser thinking it works like an Option Contract, it is far from the standard Option Contract, which we will discuss later.

Corporate Treasurers and CFOs like Forward Contracts because they seem easy to do, require no money upfront, and the exchange rate is the market rate for that day in the future. (At least they said it was the exchange rate.) The downside of a Forward Contract is that it is an agreement between two parties without the protection of an exchange. The quoted rate is the rate that the counterparty financial institution sets based on the level of risk they are willing to take on for this transaction. This usually leads to building enough profit to cover a move against them in the currency market. If the market does not move against them, then their profit is very good, and if the market moves in their favor, their gain can be exceptional. For larger Forward Contracts, financial institutions tend to use options to hedge their currency market position. That means the financial institution has built-in a profit that you cannot calculate.

Forward Contracts are private agreements between two parties. This can lead to many problems if the financial institution that wrote the contract had financial problems of its own and cannot deliver on the contract date. This is another reason that exchange-traded instruments can be better protection for the company. Exchanges have clearinghouses that guarantee delivery on the date the instrument settles. Another issue is that a Forward Contract has a fixed date. If you, for some reason, want out of the Forward Contract early, the amount it will cost you to end the contract early is determined by that institution and not subject to any market conditions. The financial institution can also refuse to let the company out of the contract, insisting that it end on its established expiration date.

The main problem with using Forward Contracts for most companies is that they consider hedging their currency risk only to be clerical work. They assign a junior accountant to establish the Forward Contract when the CFO says a hedge is needed. This person will call their bank, and he or she will then speak to another low-level bank employee. Unfortunately, without understanding the currency market, this clerk will price the Forward Contract based on numbers given by the bank's currency risk department. Only after one of these Forward Contracts moves against the company will they start asking questions and hopefully start looking at alternative derivatives.

Case Study:

This example will show how wrong the above logic can be and how much money this *"Free Service"* can really cost.

I was working with another large private Mexican conglomerate. One of the companies they owned was the equivalent of a big-box chain in the United States. An election was coming up, and they wanted to hedge $30M for 90 days and $60M for 180 days. The reason for this protection is that almost everything bought was from the United States and had to be paid for in US Dollars. All their sales came from Mexico in Pesos. They believed that if one candidate were elected, the Peso would take a big haircut, thus devaluing the Peso in relation to the United States Dollar. They insisted on a Forward Contract *even after* I explained the advantages of a few other types of instruments, which could be used to do the same thing. They said they had used Forward Contracts in the past, and they liked that they did not have to pay anything when they signed the contract.

The election went in their favor. The exchange rate for the Peso/Dollar did not change much, so the Forward Contract was not needed. <u>Here is where they learned all about the details of a Forward Contract.</u> There is no required payment when you sign a Forward Contract because the exchange rate for the contract is stated in the agreement. They may or may not let you out early, or they may or may not let you get a better rate. In this situation, because the Peso actually moved in favor of Mexico but against the Forward Contract, the company started to get daily margin calls. This is something they thought could never happen.

The result of this Forward Contract was that the company had to pay the financial institution $2,700,000 USD to get out of the Forward Contract.

Right after the bank wrote the Forward Contract, the bank most likely put on an Option Strategy that ensured that they had a minimal risk in this transaction no matter what happened to the exchange rate between the Peso and the US Dollar. I offered to create an Option Strategy for the company instead of the Forward Contract, but they did not want to pay anything upfront. As you will learn later in the Options Section, the option most likely would have cost them nothing if they used a Collar Strategy, but they held firm in how they wanted to move forward.

Key issues to keep in mind when considering the use of Forward Contracts to hedge the company's currency risk are:

- A Forward Contract is an instrument used to lock in a specific exchange rate for a currency pair on a particular date in the future.

- The advantage of using a Forward Contract is that if the exchange rate for the currency pair in question moves adversely against the company, there is no loss due to the difference in the exchange rate over time.

- One of the disadvantages is that, if the market moves favorably for the position, the financial institution, not the company, makes the profit that the transaction produced.

- Currency Forward Contracts can have maturity dates a month from the transaction date up to several years after that. The longer the time period, the more risk the financial institution will take on and, in doing so, will have the additional expense of hedging the same currency risk the Forward Contract is protecting.

- Currency Forwards are traded in the over-the-counter market. The price of the forward includes a profit margin for the dealer of the Forward Contract as a fee for the transaction. This profit or fee is not disclosed, so the purchaser of the Forward Contact has no idea how much profit for the institution is built into the Forward Contract the day it is written.

- Pricing the Forward Contract

    o All-in = Spot Price +/- Forward Points

        ▪ The Forward Points are based on the interest rate differential between the two currencies. Besides, the financial institution's profit is built-in along with any additional expenses the institution might have taken on, such as the cost of their option hedge.

- *Flexible Forwards (Option-Dated Forwards)*

    These allow companies a range of dates in the future, or multiple specific dates in the future, to close out of the Forward.

- *Advantage*

    The upside for using this type of Forward Contract is that if the company cannot give the exact date of maturity for the Forward Contract, the company will have the flexibility to change the date as the first maturity date approaches.

- *Disadvantage*

    The downside is that all of the dates will be priced at the best price for the financial institution when the Forward Contract originated. This also means the worst price for the company.

Closing Out of a Forward Contract

A day or two before the maturity date, the company calls the financial institution and picks one of three options for when the transaction expires:

1. Undertake the delivery as had been planned

2. Buy/Sell an off-setting contract

3. Extend the contract beyond the initial date of maturity at the new spot-rate

Negotiating:

Learning how to negotiate a Forward Contract is going to take some time. Forward Contracts are just a negotiated contract between two parties. There are no systems that display quotes for forwards.

Each contract is different. Here are some things to keep in mind:

- ✓ What is the amount of the contract?
- ✓ What are the two currencies?
- ✓ Which currency is buying the other?
- ✓ What is the length of time the contract is open?
- ✓ Does the contract have any *"early out clause"* that you can use to end the agreement early if the market moves against you, and what will it cost to exit early?
- ✓ **And the most important part of the contract is: what is the exchange rate at the end of the contract?**

Banks like to make Forward Contracts since they are so easy to do. Just sign your name, and you're covered. What does that mean? The contract creates some assumptions - the most obvious one is what direction the bank believes the market will move in and how fast they see the market moving? The goal of the Forward Contract is to lock in an exit price that will protect you if the market moves.

The first issue is, how does the bank price this kind of coverage? The bank's goal is to take no risk and to make a profit no matter what happens in the Foreign Exchange Market. This is much the same reason you're buying the Forward Contract.

So how does a contract that protects you guarantee a bank that they will make money at no risk? The Forward Contract only guarantees them a profit if the market moves in their direction, but less than they expect it to. The way the bank protects this position is to execute a currency Option Collar that will cost them very little, and if done right, will cost nothing and yet give them real protection outside of the range that is acceptable to the bank. We will discuss Collars later, but I do not see why you would not just do a Collar yourself for all that can go wrong with a Forward Contract.

Foreign Exchange Futures

Futures are a great hedge, but size does matter

Currency Futures, Forex Futures, or Foreign Exchange Futures are exchange-traded instruments that are Futures Contracts to buy or sell a specified amount of one currency at a set price at a date in the future. Like all exchange-traded futures, these Currency Futures have the added protection of being backed by the Exchange and settled by the Exchanges Clearinghouses. Currency Futures were introduced by the Chicago Mercantile Exchange (CME) in 1972, soon after the fixed exchange rate system and the gold standard was terminated. Currency Futures are traded the same as other Future Contracts on the CME. They trade in terms of contract months with standard maturity dates typically falling on the third Wednesday of

March, June, September, and December.

The CME offers a wide range of Currency Futures to companies that do business internationally. The most popular Currency Futures Contract is the EUR/USD (Euro/US Dollar). All of the major currencies have futures contracts that can be used to hedge currency risk in that country, as well as in emerging market currency pairs such as PLN/USD (Polish Zloty/US Dollar) and the RUB/USD (Russian Ruble/US Dollar).

One crucial factor to keep in mind is that not all Currency Futures Contracts trade with the same liquidity level. Less liquidity in a contract will add to the spread quoted for that pair. For example, the EUR/USD contract trades at over 400,000 contracts daily versus the BRL/USD (Brazilian Real/US Dollar) that trades at about 30 contracts a day. The CME offers 49 Currency Futures contracts with over $100 billion in daily liquidity, making it the world's largest regulated currency futures exchange. There are smaller exchanges such as the NYSE Euronext, the Tokyo Financial Exchange (TFX), and the Brazilian Mercantile and Futures Exchange (BM&F).

Unlike the Spot Market, where trades are made through financial institutions, Currency Futures are traded on a regulated, licensed exchange. The advantages of using exchange-traded instruments for hedging include the fact that Exchanges are regulated in terms of centralized pricing and clearing. The price of an exchange-traded instrument will be the same regardless of which broker or financial institution you use to place the trade.

Contract Specifications

All Futures Contracts must list specifications that include the contract's size, the minimum price increment, and the corresponding tick value. As with all Futures Contracts specifications, these specifications provide traders with the information they need to determine position sizing and customer account requirements. These specifications make it clear how to calculate profit and loss based on price movement.

For example, the Euro/US Dollar (EUR/USD) shows a minimum price increment of 0.0001 and a ***tick value*** of $12.50. This means that every time there is a price movement in the Euro of 0.0001, the Futures Contract's value will change by $12.50 depending on the direction of the price change in the underlying pair (EUR/USD).

Settling Currency Futures trades can be done in two ways. In most cases, the buyers and sellers will offset their original positions before the last day of trading by taking an opposite position. This trade will lead to the closing of the original Futures Contract resulting in a profit or loss in the trading account.

A less frequently used technique is used when the Futures Contract is held until the maturity or expiration date. Most of the time, this will require a physical delivery, which happens four times a year. If the company chooses this as the way they wish to settle the trade, the company, as well as the Exchange and the counterparty to the trade, are all required to complete the delivery.

In the case of trades executed on the CME, the CME has established banking relationships in the United States as well as each country represented by its Currency Futures Contracts. These banks are known as **Agent Banks** and act on behalf of the CME and maintain US Dollar accounts as well as foreign currency accounts to accommodate physical deliveries.

An essential aspect of these types of trades is that the company would have a contract with a clearinghouse instead of the counterparty to the trade. This will significantly reduce the company's risk if the counterparty failed to meet the contract's terms.

Advantages of Futures Contracts:

- o The Exchanges predetermine the size of the contracts and their expiration dates.

    - With a Futures Contract, the hedger locks in an exchange rate.

    - For Futures Contracts, the company uses a broker or an FCM instead of using a credit line from a financial institution as they would need to do with a Forward Contract.

    - The company does have to make the margin requirement and additionally pay a commission using Futures Contracts.

- A key feature of using Futures Contracts is the clearing corporation's guarantee, which takes on the counterparties' exposure. This protection is even more important when the counterparty currency is from a country with substantial risk related to political or economic factors.

An Example of a Euro Futures Contract

Negotiating:

Foreign Exchange Futures are traded on many Exchanges around the world. The most liquid Exchange is the Chicago Mercantile Exchange (CME). Using exchange-traded futures contracts gives you the ability to have the quote you get from your broker to be the same as any other broker would provide you. The Exchange will always make sure there is an actual two-sided market. This means that no matter what is going on, there will always be a bid and an ask, which will be backed by a trader and the Exchange. This is not true in the Spot Market.

What you can negotiate with futures contracts is the commission that you pay per contract. The difference in commissions can be very costly. Shopping commissions is always a good idea. The next part of your search for a Futures Broker is their experience with trading the currency markets. Most futures brokers are very familiar with the ag or agricultural commodities because that is where the volume is in this market. The next most active is the interest rate futures. These also have a sizeable active trading community. Currency Futures are very far down the line, so the number of brokers that work for firms that truly understand this market is minimal.

To give you an example, I had a large client from Mexico who visited me and wanted to go to the trading floor. I took him over to the CME. I had a friend who traded on the floor, and he walked with us and answered any of our questions. My client really wanted to see the Peso Pit, and that brought a smile to our faces. He stood in front of the pit, and we said, *"Here you go. Here is the Peso Pit'*. One guy was sitting on one of the tiers reading the newspaper. My client asked where all the trading was happening. I pointed to a computer terminal and said: "In there, it's all electronic now."

Futures Contracts have a couple of drawbacks: they are expensive and very large, much larger than most companies need to hedge their positions. If your position is substantial, you need multiple Futures Contracts, and eventually, you will have more of a hedge than you really need.

The good news is they are very safe, and they are only expensive if you do not need them. If the market moves and your futures contracts are in the money, they look like the best deal in town.

The key to effectively using a Futures Contract as a hedge is to work with a knowledgeable broker who knows the currency market as it relates to futures and has the trading experience to help you with putting together your strategy.

An Insider's Guide to Currency Hedging and Conversions

Foreign Exchange Swaps

These are what the big boys use to hedge currencies

Foreign Exchange Swaps are transactions made between two parties to exchange an equivalent amount of money with each other but in different currencies. The basic premise for this type of transaction is that parties are essentially loaning each other money and will repay the amounts at a specified date and exchange rate. This is usually done as a hedge to protect against exchange rate changes or to reduce the cost of borrowing in a foreign currency.

Most Foreign Exchange Swaps are completed between financial institutions for their own accounts or on behalf of a non-financial corporate client, such as an auto company. Foreign Exchange Swaps account for a large majority of the daily transaction volume in the global Foreign Exchange Market, according to the Bank of International Settlements.

A Foreign Exchange Swap is a transaction between two financial institutions agreeing to exchange two currencies for a specific amount of time and, in the end, exchange back the currencies at a set exchange rate. For example, one party to the trade receives 100 million British pounds (GBP) while the other $125 million (USD). This implies that the GBP/USD exchange rate is 1.25. At the end of the contract, the two financial institutions swap again at the rate stated in the Swap Contract closing the transaction.

Foreign Exchange Swaps can be relatively short, a few months, or they can last for years. During this contract period, the exchange rate can change dramatically because of one nation's political or economic situation over the Swap Contract's life. This is one of the main reason's institutions use Foreign Exchange Swaps. With a Foreign Exchange Swap, both parties know exactly how much they will have to pay out or receive on a date in the future.

An excellent example of this is when a company has to borrow money in a particular currency, and they expect the currency to strengthen significantly over the life of this agreement. A Foreign Exchange Swap will help limit the cost of repaying that borrowed currency.

What are Foreign Exchange Swaps – How do they work?

- Swaps are an instrument used to manage exposure in various currencies – typically by large financial institutions.

- Two transactions are performed simultaneously. The difference between these two on the forward's maturity date is the hedging institution's profit or loss.

    - 1) The Spot Transaction

    - 2) The Forward Transaction

- A good time to use a Foreign Exchange Swap is when the company has a known transaction with an uncertain maturity date.

- A Foreign Exchange Swap offers the company the protection of a Forward Contract with the flexibility of changing the maturity date.

- Foreign Exchange Swaps are done in two ways

    - Spot Purchase + Forward Sale

    - Spot Sale + Forward Purchase

- ✓ <u>Both the Spot Purchase and Forward Sale must be completed at the same time. If not, it is impossible to hedge the position for the Currency Swap completely.</u>

Swap Rates

- The difference between the Spot Rate and the Forward Rate is the Forward Points

- Forward Points reflect the difference between the interest rates of the two currencies

    o If the Forward Rate is lower than the Spot Rate, the counterparty buying the base currency spot and selling it forward will make a loss equal to the Swap Points and is said to *<u>pay the points</u>*

    o If the counterparty selling the base currency spot and buying it forward, he then makes a profit or is said to *<u>make the points</u>*

Foreign Exchange Options

For a true zero cost hedge or an exotic option, you need to know how to use both

George Soros, who is well known for trading currencies, especially the one British Pound trade that made him a billionaire, expressed his views on *"Foreign Exchange Options"* as:

"The economic equivalent of crack cocaine."

A Foreign Exchange Option or Currency Option is a contract that states:

The buyer has the right, but not the obligation, to buy or sell a specific currency at a specified exchange rate on or before a particular date.

For this right, the buyer pays a premium to the seller. The premium paid for an option can be high in relation to other instruments used for hedging currency risk. The premium paid depends on the strike price and the expiration date of the option. Foreign Exchange Options cannot be traded once an option is bought - all the company can do is sell it to close the position.

Foreign Exchange Options are among the most used instruments for corporations, financial institutions, or individuals to hedge currency risk against an adverse exchange rate movement. These options are derivatives based on the underlying currency.

Options Basics

There are two main types of options - **Calls and Puts**.

A company can hedge its currency risk by buying a **Call** or **Put Option**. A Foreign Exchange Option is a derivative based on the price of the underlining currency. Numerous option strategies can be employed to hedge a company's currency risk. One of the main reasons companies use Foreign Exchange Options is their limited downside risk. This risk is limited to the company's amount of money to buy the option, but the good news is that this same option strategy can have unlimited upside potential for profits.

Call Options provide the holder the right, but not the obligation, to purchase an underlying currency at a specified price, the strike price, for a certain period of time. If the currency exchange price fails to meet the strike price before the expiration date, the option expires worthless. A call option on a currency is purchased to protect the company against a rise in the counterparty currency. The company would use its profit on the option trade to cover the loss from the currency move.

Put Options also give the company the right but not the obligation to sell the underlying currency at a specified price, the strike price, for a certain period. As with a call option, if the option price does not hit the strike price, the option expires worthless. Put Options are used if the company believes the other currency will lose value over the time of the transaction. In most cases, this would be good for the company. However, with a Put Option, the company can profit from the move down.

Foreign Exchange Options - Styles

- American-Style Options

  - They are exercisable before the expiration date.

- European-Style Options

  - They are only exercisable on the expiration date.

- Asian-Style Options (Average Rate Options)

  - Their payoff is dependent upon the average exchange rate during the term of the option.

- Over-the-Counter Options

  - Their contract size, expiration date, and strike price are tailored to the hedger's needs.

- Exchange-traded Options

  - The exchange standardizes their contract size, expiration date, and strike price.

Currency Options are used to protect the downside risk of a long-term multinational transaction. A firm bid on a major multi-year project can use options to limit the downside risk over time.

A firm can use an option instead of a forward to protect against the downside risk while benefiting from an upside move.

Foreign Exchange Options can be used to protect against political risk. A firm can use options to protect against an anticipated fast move in the value of one currency in relation to another due to a political risk, such as the election of a new President.

Foreign Exchange Options

- ✓ They reduce the risk of adverse market moves.
- ✓ They remain potentially profitable to favorable market moves.
- ✓ Rather than having to wait until the expiration date, options can be exercised once they hit the strike price.
- ✓ FX Options trade both over the counter and on exchanges.

Foreign Exchange Options: Fundamentals

- o FX Option prices are based on:
  - ✓ Current Exchange Rates
  - ✓ Strike Rates
  - ✓ Risk-Free Foreign Investment Rates
  - ✓ Risk-Free Domestic Investment Rates
  - ✓ Option Put or Option Call
  - ✓ Time until the Expiration Date
  - ✓ Exercise Privileges
  - ✓ American, European, or Asian Style Options

Foreign Exchange Options: Premiums

- ✓ Although hedgers must pay a premium to purchase their options, an advantage the options give to the hedger is that the maximum potential for loss is that of the premium itself.

- ✓ Since option buyers benefit from the advantage of selling if the market moves in their favor – they have to pay the premium of an option to the seller.

FX Option Premiums are based on:

- o Intrinsic Value + Time Value

    - Intrinsic Value: the amount an option is in-the-money.

    - Time Value: the probability that the option will be in-the-money before the expiration date. As time passes on the option, it becomes less likely that the option will be "in-the-money" and therefore, the Time Value erodes as the expiration date nears.

Collar Option Strategy

This strategy is a common strategy for currency option hedgers. Currency options on their own can be expensive. For this reason, the Collar Option Strategy helps to lower the cost of using options to hedge a currency position.

A Collar combines the purchase of a Call Option with a Put Option sale for the same expiration date and the same currency. The strike prices are different, causing the sold option to generate an option premium to offset the purchased call options cost. If the Option Strategy is developed correctly, the purchase and sale should offset, leaving the Collar as a free trade.

There are a couple of downsides to this strategy. The first downside is the sold option might require a margin that can be expensive during a strong move in the underlying currency. The second downside is that the Collar not only protects against moves in the underlying currency but also limits the upside potential of a strong move in favor of the underlying currency.

An example of a Zero-Cost Collar Option Strategy is:

The current exchange rate for CAD/USD (Canadian Dollar/US Dollar) is 1.2500

>Buy a Call at 1.2700 CAD/USD

>Sell a Put at 1.2300 CAD/USD

Three potential scenarios can occur:

>*Scenario 1* – The Exchange Rate ends up over the 1.2700 CAD/USD. The company will exercise the Call Option and buy the USD at 1.2700 no matter how high the market goes – the Put Option expires worthless.

Scenario 2 - The exchange rate is below 1.2300. The bank will exercise the Put, and the company will be required to buy the USD from the bank at 1.2300 – the Call Option expires worthless.

Scenario 3 - If the exchange rate is between 1.2300 and 1.2700 – both Options expire worthless. The company buys the USD at the market.

Exotic Options

Robert Jarrow, a professor at Cornell University, defines an Exotic Option as: ***"Anything but vanilla."***   (*I like that one.*)

Exotic Options are a variation of the standard option contracts traded on the exchanges. The difference is that with an Exotic Option, the company can set the strike price, the price at which the option becomes exercisable, and the date the option will expire.

This type of option is a hybrid option in that it is not traded on an Exchange, but it's more like a Forward Contract; it is an option written by a financial institution. These options can be beneficial for protecting a currency position in the future using non-G10 currencies or timeframes that exceed the regular expiration schedule of an option.

By using Exotic Options, a company can build a hedge for the Namibian Dollar valued at $10,250,000 that will expire on May 10, 2024. Although these types of options are expensive, they offer a security level that is not possible anywhere else.

Exotic Options key points are:

- Exotic currency options usually involve trading less liquid currencies such as Namibian Dollars against the Russian Ruble

- Proxy Hedging Strategy

    - The hedging of related currencies: Some less commonly traded currencies that are used in neighboring countries often have a positive correlation to one another due to regional trade and cultural and political similarities.

    - *Problem:* Past positive correlations between regional currencies does not mean that there will be a positive correlation in the future. Moreover, even though two bordering countries may trade significantly more with one another than with trading partners outside of their geographical region, the relationships between their governments and the private sector can be strongly divergent (e.g., Colombia & Venezuela).

✓ Foreign Currency Debt Example:

- If a U.S. organization were to have a £10,000,000 in liability for a British transaction, a change in the exchange rate would dramatically affect its liability in USD.

An Insider's Guide to Currency Hedging and Conversions

Exchange Rate USD – GBP	Translated Liability
1.500 (approx. 2002)	$15,000,000
2.000 (approx. 2007)	$20,000,000

Negotiating:

Currency Options can be negotiated in a few different ways depending on the Option Strategy that you're employing. If you have a powerful feeling about the direction the market is moving in, you can, for example, buy the spot currency now and buy a put option to protect against a downward movement of the currency. When it's time to use the currency in a transaction, you will keep the profit from the option to make up for the movement of the currency in the market.

If you're using the Collar Strategy, you want to price the Put and Call Options, so they offset each other, and the trade costs you zero (Zero Cost Options). They give you the downside protection but limit the upside profit.

The third type of Option, and the one that I have used most of the time for large, valued positions, is an Exotic Option. These are custom options designed just for this one position. The currency, the option's size, and the strike price is set to give maximum protection without buying any more size or time than is needed.

These types of Options can only be written by a few of the largest firms. You will need either a direct connection to a major currency trading desk or a relationship with an agency currency trading desk that can shop this type of option around for you. My recommendation is to work through an agency currency trading desk. They have the contacts. This is their business, and without any way for you to verify that the price you were quoted is the best price, you have to work with traders that know this market cold.

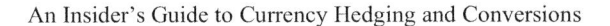

Currency Correlations

Using gold or oil to hedge your currency position

Currency correlation happens when certain currency pairs move in the same direction or the opposite direction simultaneously. When currency pairs are moving in the same direction simultaneously, they are said to be showing a positive correlation. When pairs are moving in opposite directions simultaneously, they are said to be showing a negative correlation.

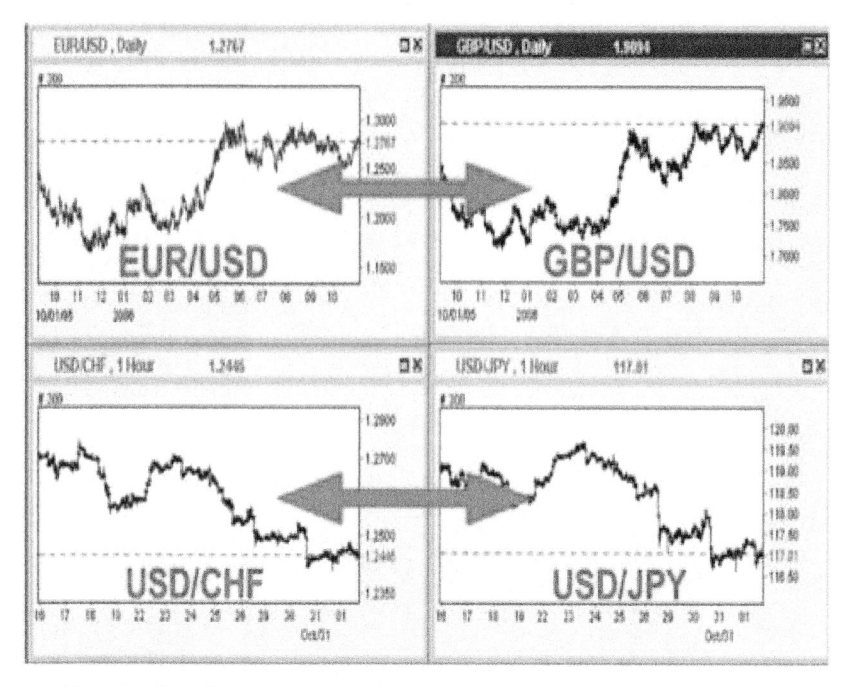

Example of currencies that are correlated to each other.

This chart shows the positive correlation between the EUR/USD pair and the GBP/USD pair. It also shows the positive correlation between the USD/CHF and the USD/JPY pairs.

Another form of correlation for currency pairs is when a currency pair positively or negatively correlates to a commodity. In these correlations, the currency pair moves with the commodity. At times the commodity will lead the currency giving the company an advantage as to what direction the currency will be moving.

An Insider's Guide to Currency Hedging and Conversions

- ✓ Aussie Dollar (AUD) moves in correlation to the price of Gold

- ✓ Canadian Dollar (CAD) moves in correlation to the price of Oil

- ✓ The Euro moves in correlation to Interest Rates

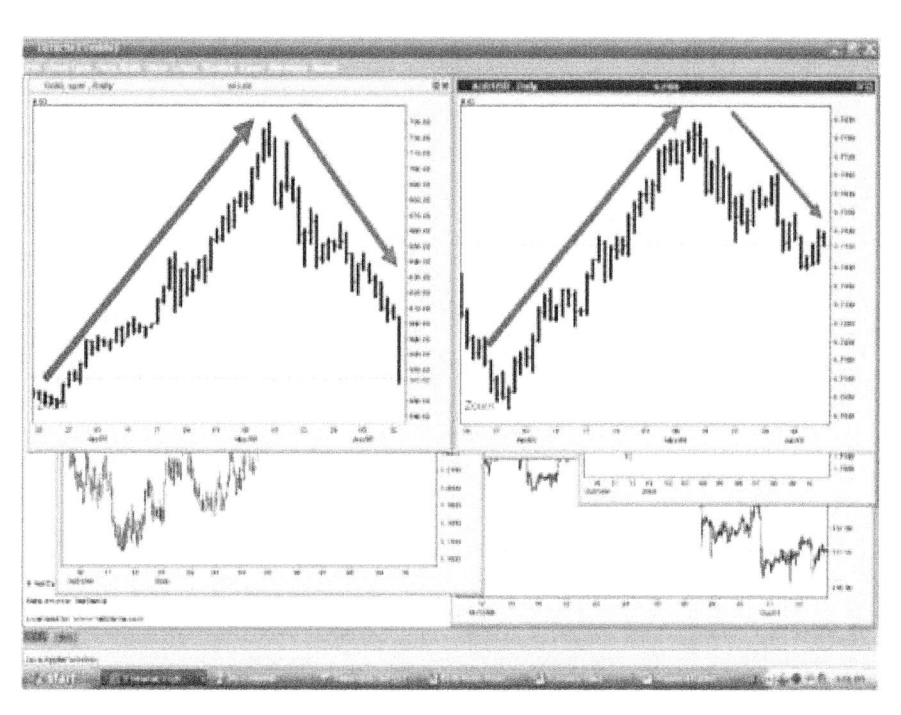

An example of how gold and the Aussie can correlate

Gold Chart / AUD Chart

An Insider's Guide to Currency Hedging and Conversions

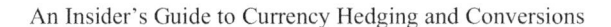

Foreign Exchange Conversion – Delivery

Currency conversion or delivery is the most profitable department in most large banks

Currency Conversion or Currency Delivery is the root of the Foreign Exchange Market. Currency Delivery is the process of converting one country's currency into another country's currency. The conversion is done based on the current exchange rate plus a markup. A company may receive less or more value after the conversion is converted based on the total of the exchange rate plus markup.

The terms Currency Delivery, Cash Settlement, or Cash Delivery are also used as a settlement procedure for futures or options contracts when they expire or are exercised. The cash settlement requires the seller of the financial instrument to transfer the associated cash position to the buyer rather than deliver the actual physical underlying currency.

Cash Settlements are always used for non-deliverable currencies. When an option or future in one of these expires or is executed, there is no way of delivering the currency involved. The difference is either paid or debited from the company account in US Dollars.

Countries with non-deliverable currencies include Russia, India, Brazil, and Chile, to name just a few. If you are not sure if the country you're planning on working with has a deliverable or non-deliverable currency, you need first to find out and see how the counterparty plans to deal with this situation.

This is the main area in the Foreign Exchange Market for the *"FREE"* service. Like I mentioned, banks will tell you that they will do your currency conversions for free because you're such a great customer. I spent many years doing *"FREE"* conversions, and we all made a lot of money doing it. There are a few parts to this free service you have to pay attention to:

- The first is that they will do the conversion at market rates. As we know now, there is no standardized Foreign Exchange Market, so there is no standardized currency conversion rate.

- The second is that as business people, we think of money with two decimal places. As you learned earlier in this book, the institutions doing the conversions think in 5 decimal places.

- The third is the most interesting to me. For instance, when you say you need 3 million Euros, they simply give you the number of US dollars they require to provide you that amount. The institution rarely gives the conversion rate used.

You would be amazed at the number of people I have met over the years that have done hundreds of these types of transactions and never worked out the exact conversion price for that transaction. Many of them said they trust their bank, and others say it must be the standard conversion ratio.

Another interesting aspect of conversions is that if you're doing the conversion through your local or regional bank or your brokerage firm, the real conversion is most likely being done by a major bank that they have a relationship with.

> *Therefore, the major bank has to make money, your local bank or brokerage firm has to make money, and you're somehow getting it all for "free???"*

For many of the major banks around the World, this is the most profitable department in the bank. It's fine that the bank makes money, but I think their profit should have some relationship to the work involved as well as the market environment at that time. You can have some fun with your bank when you call them to do a conversion, and you say you want to know the conversion amounts to the 5th decimal point. That might even confuse the person you're talking to, and if it does, just ask him to call his trading desk for an explanation.

Using the terms, understanding the market, and how it's priced will put you in a new category with your banker. They should start looking at you more as a trader than a client, which is a very good thing.

Case Study:

I have to preface this by saying that I did this investigation several years ago, so the numbers might not be the same today, but the idea of how banking is done is the same.

I wanted to see just how far apart banks in the US would be when quoting a very standardized foreign exchange conversion for a good client in Italy.

I called five of the largest US banks that I knew did a large volume of currency conversions for their clients. I told each bank that I was the CFO for a large international manufacturing firm and needed to convert $3,000,000USD to Euros once a month for at least the next two years. I also said that if we chose their bank to do the conversions that we would open an account and keep at least $5,000,000USD in that account at all times. This account could be used as collateral for the transactions, and that our company would not use these funds for anything else. By far, this conversation is one of the most straightforward conversions of any currency pairs done daily. This would seem to give the bank more than the average level of security for their risk management team to consider for each of the monthly transactions.

I will not mention the banks' names, but I assure you that they would be on the top of your list of banks to call to handle this type of transaction. They would not give me a price to do the conversion but said they do these types of transactions for their excellent customers at market rates without fees. I also never called any of the banks back to see if I could get a better exchange rate. The numbers below are just the <u>first quote</u> from each bank. I know from experience that most firms do not even realize they can negotiate to get a better exchange rate. They believe that the rate the bank gives them is the only rate, and that is why these types of transactions are handled by mid-level people who have no idea that this is an active market that can be negotiated.

To help me get an idea of what their market rates were at the time, as I said before, I asked them to quote on a 3 million Dollar conversion to Euros. Some banks gave me a quote right on the spot. Others had to call me back later in the day or even the next day. I asked them to provide me with the date and time of their quote to be fair when comparing the other banks' quotes. Most of the banks gave me a number in US Dollars that I would pay for the conversion along with the date and time of the quote. A couple of the banks said that the time would not matter because their quotes are the same all day.

After receiving the banks' quotes, I checked with our trading desk to see what price they would give me. This price would include a markup for the desk's profit on the trade. I then added $1,500 as another markup for my division.

The results were fascinating, or should I say horrifying. Even though I did several conversions daily for clients, some of these prices amazed me. The lowest cost from any of the banks had a $5,000 markup built into the conversion above the quote from our desk. And this was by far the best quote. The next quote had a $28,000 markup built into their quote. The third was $32,000. Then they really got greedy. The fourth was $74,000, and the final one was $77,000!

When they gave me their quotes, I explained again that we would have funds in their bank to cover the conversion even before they made the trade and that we would make at least 24 of these conversions over the next two years. I said that we currently worked with a bank that has been doing these types of trades for us, and we were seriously looking to replace that bank.

> *I believe that it is clear now why these banks do not want to charge a fee. How would they ever justify these types of numbers to their clients? As I mentioned earlier, to add insult to injury without them calling this markup a fee and sending the company a bill, the company lost the opportunity to deduct the markup as an expense. This made it even more expensive for the company.*

Bank Comparison Conversion Chart

Total USD converted	Total Markup	Percentage	Markup per dollar in cents	1 Year Cost	Missed Tax Deduction
$ 3,000,000	$ 5,000	0.17%	$0.00	$ 60,000	$ 21,000
$ 3,000,000	$ 28,000	0.93%	$0.00	$ 336,000	$117,600
$ 3,000,000	$ 32,000	1.07%	$0.01	$ 384,000	$134,400
$ 3,000,000	$ 74,000	2.47%	$0.02	$ 888,000	$310,800
$ 3,000,000	$ 77,000	2.57%	$0.03	$ 924,000	$323,400

Key Points to Understanding Conversion Rates

- ✓ Banks are risk adverse (well, they should be)
- ✓ Conversions rates are set first by the Foreign Exchange Trading Desk each day
- ✓ After that, they go to the banks' Risk Management Department

    o Here they must set the SPREAD for the day
    o This SPREAD must be wide enough to ensure that no matter what happens, the bank is covered
    o This new rate is what the bank calls the MARKET RATE

Case Study:

In this case study, I will discuss a new client that did a simple monthly conversion of Canadian Dollars to US Dollars. In the world of Foreign Exchange, this is by far one of the easiest, tightest spread conversions that can be done.

I contacted a major international fast-food chain that does business in the US and Canada. I spoke with the CFO of the Canadian Division, and he told me that they must convert Canadian Dollars to US Dollars every month to send to the parent company in the United States. The amount they have to send monthly is $2,500,000USD. He stated that the bank does this at market rates and does not even charge a transaction fee. He asked me how I could give him a better deal than "*free.*"

I asked him for the last date and time he converted Canadian Dollars to US Dollars. I would then price the conversion and see if my rate would be better than his bank. He thought that was a waste of time but agreed. He gave me the information that I needed, and I said I would get back to him within the hour. I called him back shortly with the exchange rate and the number of Canadian Dollars needed that day to be converted into $2,500,000USD. I added $1,500 to that number as our markup on the trade. This was a huge commission for such a simple trade, but I wanted to see how close I could get to their bank exchange rate. When I called him back and gave him my number, he said I should find a new job because I would not be working there much longer.

He thought that I was giving away money! He stated that my price was $29,000CAD (Canadian Dollars) less than what he paid.

He then told me that a large US conglomerate owned this international chain, and the same conglomerate also owned the bank that they use in the US. I asked for a few minutes to check my numbers. I then called our desk, and we rechecked the numbers, and the number that I had given him was the right number. It did include the $1,500 markup, which was, as I stated earlier, a huge profit on one of the simplest foreign exchange conversions - Canadian Dollars for US Dollars (nothing tricky there).

The CFO did call the banker he worked with and gave him the numbers I quoted, and explained that I would be doing his conversions in the future. The banker checked with others at the institution and called the CFO back and said that he could do the conversions at the same rate that I quoted in the future. He said that what he originally quoted was the standard markup that they use if no one questions the rate. He also said his bank has to make a profit, and <u>those currency conversions are one of the most profitable services in his bank.</u> Since they were both owned by the same conglomerate in the United States, he thought that it was a fair markup, *$29,000CAD for a simple trade* **(fair for whom?).**

I knew he had been doing these transactions every month for at least three years. If he had averaged an overpayment of $29,000CAD every month, he would have paid the bank over $1,000,000 more for these conversions than he would have if he checked into the rate he was paying. To make matters worse, if the bank had charged him a monthly fee of $29,000CAD, he could have at least deducted the cost as an expense on their taxes. So, because they hid the price, he not only paid an amount that he would never have agreed to, but he also lost the tax deduction for a legitimate business expense. That deduction would have saved his company between $300,000 and $400,000CAD over the three years, which made his total loss over $1,300,000CAD.

The interesting thing is that no one sees a loss on their books with the banks doing business this way, but the bank shows huge income for effortless transactions.

This scenario happened more times than I can remember. He continued working with the bank - just with much better rates going forward - thanks to me.

Negotiating:

Negotiating is one area that almost every company can improve on. However, very few even consider negotiating currency conversions a possibility. This is the transaction that bankers love; they get to say they will do it *"for free"* and then charge whatever they want without disclosing any actual prices. As long as they say the conversion was done at the market price, most firms are content thinking that they got a *"free service"* from their bank.

It's tough for the average company to know the real price of conversions. There is no actual market price because there is no Exchange to set that price and no Clearing Firm to compare the trade price to the market price. Even local and regional banks have the same problem. Most of the time, they are not making the conversion trade but are using a correspondent bank that makes the trade and tells the local bank what the market number is, not the number they made the trade at. If you're doing your conversions through local or regional banks, you have to remember that your bank needs to make money on the trade, the correspondent bank has to make money on the trade, and the counterparty to the trade has to make money on the trade. All these people make serious money on *"free trades"* - amazing.

Conclusion

Wrapping it all up

I want to make it perfectly clear that not all financial institutions are out to make a ridiculous amount of money on every transaction. I have worked with many financial institutions that provided excellent service at fair prices. The problem is that the way these transactions are structured, it is just not clear who is making what on each deal.

The goal in structuring either hedges or conversions is to understand that all of these functions are all negotiable. Not only negotiable within the institution you use now, but between several institutions. You can use one that you do Euros with, another one that you do Cable with, another one for hedging, and a different institution for conversions. That is why I wanted to make sure you understood the terminology.

It is not always easy to figure out how much money is being made by the institution just by looking at the deal. After reviewing both past and present transactions, I was able to tell some of my clients that my advice was to stay with the bank or brokerage firm they had already been working with. The deals had been good, and the service was excellent. In every one of these consulting projects, the client felt they got their money's worth because they had an independent third-party review with a consultant who agreed that their current arrangement was right for their business. Other firms who got the bad news that many of their trades were not good for their company were happy that things would be much more profitable in the future.

ONE LAST CASE STUDY:

I had a client who owned and ran a manufacturing firm in the Midwest. They produced parts for the auto industry. His father started the firm, and they had a very impressive list of customers. All the big US auto firms used them as well as a couple of European firms. The fellow who owned the company admitted that he grew up in a very comfortable family with more than enough money and no question about what he would do for a living. Growing up, his best friend was the son of his father's best friend, whose family owned the local bank. Both families stayed very close, with the fathers having dinner every Thursday night for over 30 years and the sons kept the tradition to this date having dinner every Thursday night.

Because of the business level the manufacturing firm did with European auto firms, they had to hedge their currency risk. In addition to currency hedging, they had a fair amount of currency conversions every month to bring funds back to the US and cover some European operations expenses. The friend's bank had been doing these transactions for the firm for many years. Because of their relationship, they saw no reason to do their business anywhere else. The banker had always done the business at **"MARKET RATES"** and with **"NO FEES"** *sound familiar by now?*

I met the owner at a conference I spoke at, and after my speech, there was a reception where he approached me to tell me how lucky he was that he did not have to worry about hedging because his friend made sure he got the best rates and never charged him a fee. He told me the story about growing up with the banker and their fathers' relationship, so I told him he was very fortunate to have this relationship. I asked him if he knew who the local bank was working with for the hedging and conversions? He said he thought they did it all. I said he might want to check and see if they use anyone else. It is unlikely that a small Midwest bank would have the banking and brokerage relationships to do these types of transactions directly. He said he would check and give me a call. He thanked me for my time, and then we moved on to others at the reception.

About two weeks later, the manufacturer called to tell me he had a long talk with his friend, the banker, and was not happy with what he was told. The banker did tell him that they work with a couple of large money center banks for his transactions, but his bank did all their business at the rate given to them by the larger bank and never charged him a fee. He remembered from my presentation that these types should be shopped around and negotiated. So he asked the banker if they had been doing that with his business. The banker told him that because his bank was such a good customer of the larger bank, they did everything at **"MARKET RATES"** and for a

"FREE SERVICE."

He asked me if I could check this out and make sure his bank was getting a good deal. I agreed as part of our ongoing consulting agreement to work with his banker. I asked him for the basic numbers on the last three hedges he put on, not the hedges' details, but the amount of the last three conversions they did. I needed only the amount they converted, not both sides.

Because the hedges and conversions were US Dollar/Euro, it would have been very easy to structure the hedge in the manner I was suggesting. For these three examples, I gave him our conversion rate for the dates and times he had made his conversions to compare pricing.

It turned out that the friend's bank was not such a great customer after all to their correspondent bank. The friend's bank used simple forward contracts written by the correspondent bank to hedge with a profitable rate for the correspondent bank.

When he took this information to his banker, he said that his friend was very embarrassed and had to say that he was disappointed in the fact that his friend never really checked to see if the hedges and conversions were being done at the best rates.

His banker called me, and we started doing the manufacturer's business, but in time, the local banker contacted me, and I worked with him replacing his correspondent bank for all of his conversion deals.

I hope that you now feel you can deal with the financial institutions as a peer, no longer an uneducated client that some institutions take advantage of for their own gains.

Please contact me anytime with questions or if you want to discuss a particular negotiation. I would appreciate hearing about your real-life situations and how this book helped you be a more powerful negotiator from here on out.

FXXRic@Gmail.com

An Insider's Guide to Currency Hedging and Conversions

Thank You

I sincerely want to thank you for reading my book. This subject is very complex and putting all the material into a useful and understandable form took some time. I wanted to show you how and why the Foreign Exchange Market works the way that it does and for you to get the upper hand dealing with people who have devoted their lives to this close-knit community. Hopefully, my real-life **Case Studies** helped you see the value of knowing how to negotiate like the pros and that you feel like I have laid this material out concisely so that you continue to use this book as a reference.

You should now know that you can put into practice what I have shown you and become a more valuable asset to your company. Please contact me and give me one or more of your real-world Case Studies, or just let me know how it felt to deal as a knowledgeable participant. It is always very gratifying to know that the hours spent preparing the material have been more than worth it.

If you have a few minutes, I would love to hear your thoughts on the book!

Ric Chappetto

FXXRic@Gmail.com

ABOUT THE AUTHOR

Ric Chappetto has 40 years of experience in the Financial Services Industry. For the last 20 years, he focused on the Foreign Exchange Market, providing services to corporations and institutions doing International Business requiring multi-currency transactions. During the previous 20 years, Ric held senior management positions with major Wall Street and LaSalle Street firms, holding the titles of President, Chief Operations Officer, Chief Financial Officer, and Senior Vice President.

When Ric started focusing on the Foreign Exchange Market, he learned how major financial institutions kept their clients in the dark and made huge amounts of money on transactions their clients thought the transactions were done at *"Market Rates"* and with *"No Fees."*

A major part of Ric's education in this market came from personally developing relationships in 16 countries in Europe, South America, and the Far East. Working directly with these people on-site, Ric was able to see how the Foreign Exchange Market looked from the other side. Internationally his clients included brokers, bankers, and some large clients in these countries. Ric enjoyed being able to offer them a better selection of products and superior pricing alternatives.

Ric has been a guest lecturer speaking on how the Foreign Exchange Market works at Northwestern University, the University of Chicago, the University of Illinois, and the UCLA Extension. The two-day workshop Ric developed and presented at the UCLA Extension was used as the book's outline.

Ric is an Army Veteran.

FXXRic@Gmail.com

Printed in Great Britain
by Amazon